"In a world where sustainable recovery demands daily engagement and spiritual grounding, *Recovery Minute* delivers bite-sized wisdom and actionable hope for the journey. These devotionals are more than inspiration; they're a lifeline for those choosing connection over compulsion, one day at a time."

—Dr. Jake Porter
Daring Ventures
Author, *Breaking Barriers, Building Bridges*

"*Recovery Minute* is an uplifting daily devotional that will inspire you to live your best recovery and life. This is an exciting resource from a master practitioner and pastor. Thank you, Mark!"

—Dr. Carol Sheets
"Carol the Coach"
Author, *Help Her Heal*

"Rooted in recovery and faith, Dr. Mark Denison's *Recovery Minute* provides relatable faith-based devotions for those in recovery. The devotions are practical and inspiring. I'm excited to incorporate these devotions into my morning routines and recommend them to my clients as well."

—Dr. Dan Drake, LMFT, CCPS-S, CCDG-M, CSAT-S
Intensive Recovery Healing
Co-author, *Full Disclosure* series,
Building True Intimacy,
and *Letters from a Sex Addict*

"Dr. Denison's devotions will start your day with the right focus, pointing you toward God and helping others. I highly recommend *Recovery Minute.*"

—Dr. Ben Young
Senior Pastor, Second Baptist Church
Houston, Texas
Author, *Devotions for Dating Couples*

"These quick devotionals offer practical bits of knowledge and truth. They will be a foundation of your recovery. I am grateful for this book and look forward to recommending it to all the men in my group."

—Nick Stumbo
Executive Director, Pure Desire
Author, *Safe: Creating a Culture of Grace in a Climate of Shame*

"For years, I have started my day with Mark Denison's *Recovery Minute.* His breadth of take-off topics is broad—trivia, sports, history, you name it—but his takeaways are always solid, helpful reminders. It's a quick, often thought-provoking, always positive foundation for the day."

—Marnie C. Ferree, LMFT, CSAT
Founder, Bethesda Workshops
Author, *No Stones: Women Redeemed from Sexual Addiction*

"A year's worth of daily encouragement—Dr. Mark Denison has a knack for relaying deep insights in a few short sentences that stick with you all day. You don't want to miss a single *Recovery Minute* for life's daily ups and downs."

—Sam Black
Covenant Eyes, Director of Recovery Education
Author, *The Healing Church*

"Recovery from any unwanted behavior is hard work. And there are no days off in recovery! Mark has done a masterful job of providing powerful and practical insights in this devotional. For those who want to take their recovery seriously, I recommend *Recovery Minute*. It might prove to be the most important sixty seconds of your morning."

—Jonathan Daugherty
Founder, Be Broken Ministries
Author, *Grace-Based Recovery*

"For the past four years, Mark's 90-Day *Recovery Guide* has been a trusted resource for hundreds of LSU men in our college ministry seeking freedom. This new resource provides short, daily readings that will help men confront their struggles and find lasting freedom."

—Eric Allred
Executive Pastor and Recovery Leader
The Chapel,
Baton Rouge, Louisiana

"If you're looking for a daily dose of sharp insight and biblical wisdom on recovery, *Recovery Minute* is for you. Reading a page per day is not only doable, it's enjoyable. This entertaining book can help you gain and maintain momentum, and Mark Denison is a trustworthy companion for the journey."

—Drew Boa, PSAP, BSP
Founder, Husband Material Ministries
Author, *Outgrow Porn* and *Redeemed Sexuality*

"You will be blessed reading these common sense and biblically based devotions from my friend Dr. Mark Denison. His passion to help those of us who are looking for a new beginning comes through with every passing page. These words are a wonderful reminder that it is never too late for a new beginning. Read it . . . and reap!"

—Dr. O. S. Hawkins
Former Pastor, First Baptist Church
Dallas, Texas
Author, *The Joshua Code* and *The Bible Code*

"I've heard mutual clients describe how they have made Mark Denison's comforting words a part of their daily ritual for years. After reading *Recovery Minute*, I understand why. Mark has created a recovery almanac—short, practical, bite-sized daily devotions that are a perfect fit for recovery practices."

—Dr. Janice Caudill, CSAT-S
Founding Member, APSATS
Author, *Full Disclosure: Seeking Truth After Sexual Betrayal*

"Dr. Mark has done it again! My friend has created a daily companion for anyone walking the path of recovery. With 366 days of biblically grounded wisdom, *Recovery Minute* isn't just another devotional; it's a lifeline, an immediate addition to my recommended reading list."

—Michael Leahy
Founder and Co-CEO, BraveHearts
Author, *Porn Nation*

"*Recovery Minute* is a powerful and practical guide. Each entry is brief but impactful, perfect for those seeking clarity, strength, and spiritual grounding in their healing journey. This book isn't just a devotional; it's a lifeline."

—Stan Pavlovich
Campus Pastor, Bayside Community Church
Bradenton, Florida

"Dr. Mark Denison's latest book is a remarkable collection that blends hard-earned wisdom with faith and practical tools. Each day, Mark delivers a powerful mix of historical insights, sports trivia, humor, biblical truths, and hands-on recovery strategies, all aimed at steering men and women toward Christ-centered healing."

—Tom Weaver
Founder, Come to the Table Ministry
Host, Men Make Men

"You can't live without it! The wisdom of *Recovery Minute* will encourage you, challenge you, inform you, and ultimately change you. No matter where you have been, what you have done, or what's been done to you, you will find . . . there's still hope!"

—Dr. Roger Patterson
Senior Pastor, CityRise Church
Houston, Texas
Author, *A Minute of Vision for Men*

"I'm deeply grateful that Mark has taken the time to prayerfully curate some of his most meaningful spiritual reflections into a clear and accessible daily devotional. Every addict, regardless of background, will benefit from adding this powerful resource to their daily recovery arsenal."

—Jorge Sesin
Founder and Executive Director
Castimonia Restoration Ministry

"Mark Denison is a master of getting to the point. These brief, meaningful devotions will help you start your day off right and help keep you on the road to recovery."

—David Murrow
Founder, Church for Men
Author, *Why Men Hate Going to Church*

"The genius of this book is it gives a principle for each day that you can focus on for that day's sobriety. Use it one day at a time. You'll be glad you did!"

—Dr. James Reeves
Pastor, City on a Hill
Fort Worth, Texas
Producer, *Fearless Series for Men and Women*

"In this brilliantly concise, interesting, and humorous daily devotional, Mark Denison has written a gift to every one of us in a process of recovery. Each day is packed with simple, pungent messages of truth, accompanied by a relevant scripture. Use this to start each day!"

—Garry Ingraham
Founder, Love & Truth Network

"Mark Denison has written over 3,000 daily Recovery Minute devotionals over the past several years, and this book contains the best of the best! Every day, you'll receive a nugget of wisdom that reminds you there's still hope."

—Rod Handley
Founder, Character That Counts
Author, *Character That Counts – Who's Counting Yours?*

"Powerful. Practical. Biblical. *Recovery Minute* delivers daily truth with laser focus and real-world relevance. It's not just a devotional. It's a lifeline for anyone pursuing freedom and restoration."

—Ed Young
Senior Pastor, Fellowship Church
Grapevine, Texas
New York Times Best-Selling Author

"I can't express enough how much Mark's *Recovery Minute* resonates with me! Mark has a unique way of blending personal anecdotes with powerful insights that truly enlighten the reader. His emphasis on life's struggles as invitations from God to grow and follow in the footsteps of Jesus is both uplifting and motivating."

—Jason M. Hunt, MD
Author, *Understanding Addiction: Know Science, No Stigma*

"*Recovery Minute* is the perfect supplement to a person's recovery. Each devotional only takes a few moments to read but will keep you grounded in God's truth while challenging you to go deeper and deeper in your healing journey."

—Noah Filipiak
The Flip Side Podcast
Author, *Beyond the Battle*

"Mark Denison has been a huge source of inspiration for me and the guys that I coach in my recovery group. This devotional is another great tool to providing the reader the 'breadcrumbs' they need to move forward step by step toward a better, more Christ-like future."

—Vern Tompke
Founding Pastor, Chilliwack Vineyard Church
Chilliwack, British Columbia
Host, *Finding Traction* podcast

"Drawing from decades of personal experience and professional guidance, Mark's *Recovery Minute* offers a year's worth of daily waybread to keep us fit and alert on the path. Be nourished by his wisdom."

—Daniel Weiss
President, Sexual Integrity Leaders, Inc.
Co-author, *Treading Boldly Through a Pornographic World*

"Nothing is more important to my recovery than my daily connection with God. Mark gives a powerful and practical boost to that connection every single day. His heart for God and his wisdom for recovery make this an important tool for anyone seeking freedom and hope."

—Troy Hass, CADC II, CSAT
Founder, HopeQuest

"This book offers a beacon of hope for anyone navigating the journey of addiction recovery. I find these recovery minutes extremely helpful in my recovery pathway every day."

—Dr. James Real, Ed.D., M.Div., SATP-C
Pastor, Journey Church of the Nazarene
Kansas City, Missouri

"My friend has done it again! *Recovery Minute* puts actual events, spiritual truths, and recovery insights into daily signposts that point us in the direction of living the life we were meant to live."

—Tom Ryan
Founder, Living Integrated
Author, *Ashamed No More*

"*Recovery Minute* isn't just a great recovery devotional; it's simply a great devotional. Scripture passages are appropriately contextualized, and the reader is given a daily action item. Mark's sense of humor and love of trivia come through in every entry."

—Jason Huffman
Pastor, St. Mark's Methodist Church,
Baytown, Texas
Assistant Dean, Trinity Conference School of Ministry

"Mark's *Recovery Minute* cuts through common anxieties with short, thoughtful devotionals that remind readers of the power of simplicity and of doing the next right thing."

—Greg Oliver
Executive Director, Awaken Recovery
Host, *Awaken* Podcast

RECOVERY MINUTE

366 Daily Devotions to Jump Start Your Recovery

MARK DENISON

Author, *Jesus and the 12 Steps*

"Powerful. Practical. Biblical. Daily truth with laser focus. More than a devotional. It's a lifeline."

Pastor Ed Young, New York Times Best-Selling Author

LUCIDBOOKS

Recovery Minute: 366 Daily Devotions to Jump Start Your Recovery

Published by Lucid Books in Houston, TX
www.LucidBooks.com

ISBN: 978-1-63296-933-0
eISBN: 978-1-63296-934-7

Special Sales: Most Lucid Books titles are available in special quantity discounts. Custom imprinting or excerpting can also be done to fit special needs. Contact Lucid Books at Info@LucidBooks.com

To Don Haley, godly businessman, church leader, and rancher. It was my highest honor to be his pastor and friend. Don inspired me to deepen my walk with Jesus. His ninety-five years (1930–2025) seemed much too short.

CONTENTS

INTRODUCTION

After my thirty-one fruitful years of ministry as a senior pastor, God directed my wife, Beth, and me to launch a recovery ministry—There's Still Hope—for those who struggle with compulsive behaviors, specifically in the area of unwanted sexual addictions. Since the ministry began in 2017, we have seen it grow into an international ministry whose reach is touching thousands of men and women in at least twenty-five countries around the world.

The ministry provides groups every day of the week, as well as an acclaimed 90-Day Recovery Program and coaching for women. The ministry has also produced a dozen books, and we have been blessed to be featured in dozens of podcasts and publications. From the beginning, we stepped into a space that set us apart.

RECOVERY MINUTE

Every day I write a devotion that is sent by email all around the globe. From 2017 until the publication of this book, the ministry has produced over 3,000 daily Recovery Minutes, never missing a single day. This devotional book has captured what we believe are the 366 most impactful of those 3,000 devotions.

Each reading is short, interesting (we hope), and biblical. They are for men and women who struggle with any addictive behaviors, either substance or behavioral. Each Recovery Minute concludes with a simple action step—called the Recovery Step—for the day.

Included on these pages are references from all sixty-six books of the Bible. Each Recovery Minute contains at least one biblical reference, recognizing the Bible as the greatest book on recovery ever written.

This book has been a work in progress for eight years. If you are looking for historical facts, sports trivia, pithy humor, biblical exposition, or practical recovery tools, it's all here. If these daily Recovery Minutes are half the blessing to you as you read them as they were to me as I wrote them, I will have achieved my mission.

JANUARY

To fall in love with God is the greatest romance;
to seek him the greatest adventure;
to find him, the greatest human achievement.

—Saint Augustine

New Year's Day Resolutions

JANUARY 1

This is the day we all make promises for the coming year. But I say, forget the next year. Let's talk about the next twenty-four hours.

We can do a lot in a day.

In one day in 1993, Charles Servizio did 46,001 pushups. In one day, Ben Feldman sold $20 million of insurance. In one day, Will Ferrell played for ten Major League Baseball teams. (It was spring training.) In one day, the Girl Scouts bake 4.5 million thin mints.

Jesus warned, "So don't worry about tomorrow, for tomorrow will bring its own worries" (Matt. 6:34 NLT).

It's great to set goals for the next year. But it's better to set goals for the next day. Then, when you get out of bed tomorrow, do it all over again.

Recovery Step: Anyone can make a New Year's resolution. I suggest you make a New Day's resolution instead.

#1 Cause of Relapse

JANUARY 2

The Promises Treatment Center has identified seven leading signs of a relapse in sobriety. Topping the list is this: letting up on new habits.

There is no silver bullet for recovery. It is all about doing the work, day in and day out.

There's an old joke about the farmer who was struggling to produce a good crop. He prayed, and God wrote two letters across the sky: PC. The man assumed God was saying, "Preach Christ," so he built a pulpit at his farm and began preaching to all who came his way. When his crop continued to fail, he sought God again. He said, "I preached Christ! What more do you want me to do?" God replied, "By PC I didn't mean to preach Christ. I was telling you to plant corn."

The man closest to Jesus wrote, "Watch out that you do not lose what we have worked so hard to achieve. Be diligent so that you receive your full reward" (2 John 1:8 NLT).

Recovery is hard work, day in and day out. It's about establishing new habits and then sticking to the plan every day for the rest of your life.

Recovery Step: To maintain sobriety, you must do two things: establish new habits and then stick to the plan.

Recovery Cycle

JANUARY 3

In his groundbreaking work *Out of the Shadows,* Dr. Patrick Carnes identified the now-famous addiction cycle. The four phases of addiction are fantasy, ritual, acting out, and shame. For those active in their addiction, this becomes a predictable, repetitive roller-coaster ride from which there appears to be no escape.

But there is an escape. Dr. Mark Laaser has offered a Christian perspective. He has created what he calls the "recovery cycle." It, too, has four phases: vision, healthy decisions, healthy behavior, and joy.

One of the great leaders in Israel's history was Samuel. Early in life, he discovered the process of growth. "And the boy Samuel continued to grow in stature and in favor with the Lord and with people" (1 Sam. 2:26).

Like Samuel, you are growing. You are either growing in your addiction or you are growing in your recovery.

Recovery Step: Which cycle are you on: addiction or recovery? Get off the crazy train and embrace the gift of sobriety—one day and one choice at a time.

The Wright Brothers' Secret Plane

JANUARY 4

On October 5, 1905, Wilbur Wright set a world record by flying 24 miles in just thirty-nine minutes. The record stood for three more years. In order to prevent competitors from discovering their secrets to flights of such length and speed, the Wright brothers disassembled the airplane on November 7, 1905.

It is amazing the lengths we will go to in order to protect our secrets.

I say it a lot: Addiction cripples, but secrets kill. I have seen this play out hundreds of times. Let's consider just a few problems that result from keeping secrets.

- Secrets shield you from experiencing grace.
- Secrets force you into a life of isolation.
- Secrets drain you of energy for daily life.

Recovery Step: Someone needs to know your secrets. Otherwise, there will be a price to pay. "God will judge the secrets of men" (Rom. 2:16 NASB1995).

Lots-of-Stuff

JANUARY 5

There once lived a man in a faraway place that had so much stuff that they called it Stuffland. And this man had more stuff than anyone else. So they called him Lots-of-Stuff. He earned his stuff the old-fashioned way through self-reliance and hard work. Then he heard about a new place with even more stuff. They called it New Stuffland. Lots-of-Stuff had to see it for himself, so he traveled to New Stuffland. And sure enough, he saw more stuff than he ever imagined.

Then a stranger approached, offering Lots-of-Stuff more stuff than he had ever seen. But he could only keep it on one condition. He had to give it away. And miraculously, the more stuff Lots-of-Stuff gave away, the more he got back.

The stranger in this parable is Jesus Christ. The "stuff" represents sobriety, and Lots-of-Stuff is you and me.

Recovery is not a reward for hard work and brilliance; it is a gift. But you cannot receive this gift until you meet the Giver and commit to giving it away to others.

Jesus came "to seek and to save the lost" (Luke 19:10). The next step is yours.

Recovery Step: You may have lots of stuff. You may even have lots of sobriety. But if you want the lasting gift of recovery, you must do two things: meet the Giver and share the gift with others.

Five Signs of Addiction

JANUARY 6

The *Diagnostic and Statistical Manual of Mental Disorders, Fifth Edition* (DSM-5) identifies five signs that you are likely an addict.

- You are engaging in a destructive behavior longer than you intended to.
- You have made unsuccessful attempts to stop.
- Your habit has affected daily routines and responsibilities.
- You continue the activity despite negative consequences.
- Your cravings have escalated.

The first time I read this, I checked all five boxes. I'm guessing you will as well. But the good news is that there is a God who can help, who can lead you out of this wilderness.

Recovery Step: "Call on me in the day of trouble" (Ps. 50:15).

Time to Fly

JANUARY 7

Larry Walters wanted to fly. It was his greatest passion and dream. Not born with wings, he had to become rather creative, so he hitched up forty-five helium-filled balloons to his lawn chair. He strapped himself in with a snack, a soft drink, and a pellet gun. His plan was to rise 30 feet into the air and then shoot the balloons to bring about a slow, gentle landing.

He overshot his target. Larry's lawn chair rocketed to heights of 16,000 feet. He then shot his balloons until he landed on some power lines. When arrested, he told the police, "A man can't just sit there."

We really can be free! We can fly—above circumstances, temptations, and our past. But it starts with a passion to go where we have not been and do what we have not tried.

God said it like this, speaking to Abram: "The Lord had said to Abram, 'Go from your country, your people and your father's household to the land I will show you'" (Gen. 12:1).

God has big plans. You've been grounded by your addiction long enough. It's time to fly.

Recovery Step: Pray for the impossible. Pray for a life free from the bondage of addiction and for the freedom to fly above it all. Then seek God with everything you've got.

T + O = T

JANUARY 8

Temptation plus opportunity equals trouble.

Let's break that down.

Temptation: We know that some temptation is inevitable. It shows up in unavoidable images, memories, and various triggers. But we need to steer clear of temptation whenever possible. "Each person is tempted when they are dragged away by their own evil desire and enticed. Then, after desire has conceived, it gives birth to sin; and sin, when it is full-grown, gives birth to death" (James 1:14–15).

Opportunity: You need to be aware of the opportunities that are most threatening. They may include being alone at night, certain movie channels, places, people, or other situations in which you have acted out in the past.

Trouble: Put temptation and opportunity on the same page, and that chapter often ends badly. The key is to avoid temptations when you are in certain opportune moments and minimize opportunities when temptations arise.

Recovery Step: Some level of temptations and opportunities are going to happen. Do your best to not let them happen at the same time because that spells trouble.

Titanic Survivor's Tragic Death

JANUARY 9

On April 10, 1912, the *Titanic* left Southampton on her maiden voyage. Five days later, the unsinkable did the unthinkable. The *Titanic* hit an iceberg and sank, and 1,503 lives were lost; 705 survived. Let's talk about one of those survivors.

The wealthiest passengers had secured first-class tickets. They were given first access to the lifeboats when the ship began to go down. One such family was the Speddens. Frederic and Daisy occupied cabin E-40 along with their only son, six-year-old Douglas, as well as his personal nanny.

Douglas was one of the few children in first class. Most of the other 200 children perished in the icy waters. Douglas was a child of privilege. But good fortune yielded to tragedy just three years later. On August 6, 1915, Douglas was killed in the first fatal automobile accident in Maine near the family's vacation home.

Like Douglas, you may be a survivor. But victory today is no guarantee of survival tomorrow.

Paul told the church, "Even if you think you can stand up to temptation, be careful not to fall" (1 Cor. 10:12 CEV).

Recovery Step: Don't be overconfident. Thank God for yesterday's victories and today's sobriety. But stay humble and hungry because tomorrow is another day.

Lesson from Albert

JANUARY 10

I'm not a student of Albert Einstein, nor do I have evidence that he battled addictions. But he said something that every addict should embrace. It is one of the most important principles in recovery from any addiction or destructive habit.

"No problem can be solved," said Einstein, "from the same level of consciousness that created it."

As you hear it said in recovery groups, "It is your stinking thinking that got you here." We will never find sobriety until we reverse this approach.

The prophet Isaiah warned, "Woe to those who are wise in their own eyes" (Isa. 5:21).

So how, exactly, do we move beyond our own flawed thinking and embrace a new way of life? I suggest three things.

1. Be pliable.
2. Be teachable.
3. Be breakable.

Recovery Step: As you move forward with your recovery, be pliable, teachable, and breakable. The result will be a lasting sobriety you have never known.

Jesus Is Watching You

JANUARY 11

Before you act out again, ask yourself this question: What message will this send to others?

A man broke into a house late one night. The owner's parrot said to him, "Jesus is watching you." The burglar was undeterred. "What is Jesus going to do to stop me?" he asked the bird. As the man continued to fill his sack with valuables, the parrot repeated, "Jesus is watching you." This only emboldened the thief, who told the bird, "Tell Jesus he can do what he wants, and I'll take what I want."

"Okay," said, the bird. "But I warned you."

Then the parrot turned to the Doberman Pinscher who the family had named "Jesus." The parrot said, "Sic him, Jesus!"

Every time you take something that isn't yours—a glance, an image, a fantasy—Jesus is watching you. And other people are watching you too. C. S. Lewis said it well: "When we Christians behave badly, or fail to behave well we are making Christianity unbelievable to the outside world."

The antidote: "So I strive always to keep my conscience clear before God and man" (Acts 24:16).

Recovery Step: The next time you think about doing something dumb, remember two things: (a) Jesus is watching you, and (b) so is someone else.

Five Frogs on a Log

JANUARY 12

Five frogs sat on a log. Three decided to jump off. How many remained on the log? Answer: five. Here's the thing. Deciding to do something and actually doing it aren't the same thing.

A million times I decided to stop acting out in my addiction. But I didn't really stop. Why? Because decision and action are two different things.

James warned his readers, "Do not merely listen to the word, and so deceive yourselves. Do what it says" (James 1:22).

Zig Ziglar said, "It was character that got us out of bed, commitment that moved us into action, and discipline that enabled us to follow through."

Every addict needs that discipline. Decide to be sober and in recovery. Then do something about it. Follow through—go to meetings, pray, get a sponsor, seek God daily.

Are you ready for real recovery? Then get off the log. It's time to jump!

Recovery Step: Do today what you said you would do yesterday.

Leaky Cisterns

JANUARY 13

"They have forsaken me, the fountain of living waters, and hewed out cisterns for themselves, broken cisterns that can hold no water" (Jer. 2:13 ESV).

Do your cisterns hold water?

The only way your cisterns are guaranteed to hold water is if you turn to the leak-preventer every day. Jonathan Edwards said it well: "How can you expect to dwell with God forever, if you so neglect and forsake him here?"

When we seek the fountain of living water, we find our cisterns overflowing with the abundance of God's blessings. We live our lives—and our recovery—on a whole new level. We become the man or woman described by A. W. Tozer when he said, "A real Christian . . . sees the invisible, hears the inaudible, and knows that which passeth knowledge."

Recovery Step: If your cistern has a leak, bring it to God. If it is full, keep coming back to the fountain of living water every single day.

Babe Ruth's $20 Ball

JANUARY 14

"Again, the kingdom of heaven is like a merchant looking for fine pearls. When he found one of great value, he went away and sold everything he had and bought it" (Matt. 13:45–46).

In 1934, Babe Ruth launched his 700th career home run completely out of the stadium in Detroit. A 17-year-old boy named Lenny Beals retrieved the ball from under a car in the stadium parking lot. An usher escorted Lenny into the stadium where he met the Babe after the game. Ruth offered the boy $20 for the ball. The lad agreed. That ball would now be worth about $1 million.

At least Lenny kept the $20 bill. His family still has it, ninety years later.

But I'm pretty sure Lenny's family would have preferred that he kept the ball. Lenny did what most of us do. The $20 looked good in the moment. After all, in today's dollars, that would be about $400. That was a lot of money. So Lenny went for the immediate pleasure of $20 rather than the long-term benefit of owning such a rare treasure.

That's why so many people are mired in their addictions. They trade what they want most for what they want now.

Recovery Step: Trade up, from the immediate pleasure to lasting peace.

Lucky

JANUARY 15

I heard about a newspaper advertisement. It read, "Lost: one dog. Very little hair on his body. Right leg broken in auto accident. Bad left hip. Walks with a limp. Right eye missing. Left ear bitten off by another dog. Answers to the name Lucky."

One of the most common things we say to one another is "good luck." I like the way British politician Lain Duncan Smith said it. "Luck is great, but most of life is hard work."

Seneca was right when he said, "Luck is what happens when preparation meets opportunity."

The dog in our story is a lot like us. Crippled by years of our disease, we walk with a limp, but we must keep walking. We can't always see straight, but we keep looking forward.

Solomon said, "All hard work brings a profit, but mere talk leads only to poverty" (Prov. 14:23).

Recovery Step: Maybe your addiction has not cost you your marriage, job, or health. Consider yourself lucky. But it is only when you put in the work of real recovery that you can call yourself well.

Livin' Near the Beach

JANUARY 16

My family lives in Bradenton, Florida, six miles from the beach—green water, white sand, seagulls overhead.

In a word: paradise.

So I completely understand why people are flooding into Florida. What I don't understand is why people move there, within a 15-minute drive of the ocean, but then never go to the beach. That would be like going to the greatest burger joint in the world and then ordering tater tots, or going to a movie theater for a soft drink but not staying for the movie.

Jesus said, "I have come that they may have life, and have it to the full" (John 10:10).

In beach terms, God not only wants you to live in paradise; he wants you to enjoy paradise.

Recovery Step: Epicurus said, "Not what we have but what we enjoy, constitutes our abundance." God wants you to enjoy the abundant blessings of recovery—now.

Presidential Parrot

JANUARY 17

On June 8, 1845, America's seventh President died. A few days later, the funeral service of Andrew Jackson attracted thousands. One particular attendee was removed during the service because of his uncontrollable behavior. Throughout the service, he kept interrupting the speakers with fits of profanity.

Who was this disrespectful guest? It was the President's pet parrot.

Here's my question. Where did the bird learn this "fowl language"? Clearly, he learned it from the President himself.

There is a price to pay for the words we use. Solomon wrote, "The tongue has the power of life and death, and those who love it will eat its fruit" (Prov. 18:21).

Whatever you say, wherever you are, someone is listening. Words have impact. Remember the old rhyme we learned as children? "Sticks and stones may break my bones, but words will never hurt me." Whoever wrote that must have been deaf.

Recovery Step: Your words will do one of two things for those closest to you. They will help or they will hinder. Someone is listening. So choose your next words carefully.

Sermon on the Mound

JANUARY 18

Orel Hershiser was having a bad day. The All-Star pitcher was laboring on the mound when his manager, Tommy Lasorda, left the dugout for a brief visit. Lasorda got in Hershiser's face and proceeded to tell him what he could become as a pitcher. "You're a winner!" Lasorda said. After the manager returned to the dugout, Hershiser struck out the side.

The pitcher looks back on that as a turning point in his career. He credits Lasorda for what he calls the "Sermon on the Mound."

We all need to hear a good sermon from time to time. But the best sermon is not preached in the pulpit as often as it is in the office, on the golf course, or in the mirror.

Yes—in the mirror.

Jerry Bridges, author of *The Pursuit of Holiness*, wisely wrote, "Preach the gospel to yourself every day."

The prophet Ezekiel declared, "The righteousness of the righteous will be credited to them" (Ezek. 18:20). In other words, we must own our recovery. And we must be our own best encourager.

Recovery Step: Be encouraged today, if not by someone else then by yourself.

Rule #1

JANUARY 19

In my book *Recovery Rules*, I start with Rule #1: If you are 90 percent in, you're 100 percent out.

Case in point: King Amaziah.

"Amaziah was twenty-five years old when he became king, and he reigned in Jerusalem twenty-nine years. . . . He did what was right in the eyes of the Lord, but not wholeheartedly" (2 Chron. 25:1–2).

Amaziah was a young man when he became king. The Bible says he did right in God's eyes, but not with his whole heart. His half-hearted commitment to God became evident when he defeated the Edomites in battle and brought their gods home with him as spoils of war. King Amaziah conquered the Edomites, but their little gods conquered his heart.

This can happen to us, too, if we allow the idols of this world to conquer our hearts. Half-hearted devotion to God diminishes the effectiveness of our lives and weakens our witness to the world. How do we prevent this from happening? By being wholeheartedly committed to Christ in every area of our lives. Then we can do right in the eyes of the Lord with a whole heart and make a difference for him in this world. So I ask you now: Are you wholeheartedly sold out to Christ?

Recovery Step: Move from 90 percent to 100 percent.

Regrets

JANUARY 20

Regrets—we've all had a few. Let's talk about regrets.

According to psychologist Tom Gilovich, there is a difference between short-term and long-term regrets. In the short term, we tend to regret the mistakes we've made. But in the long term, we regret the opportunities we've missed.

The power of fear is 2.5 times greater than the power of hope. Out of our fear of failure, we often pass on opportunities of hope, in order to play it safe. These missed opportunities today become regrets tomorrow.

In recovery, it is critical that you miss as few opportunities as possible.

Recovery Step: Exercise faith. Capture every opportunity. Don't take it from me. Learn from the Master himself: "He could not do any miracles there, except lay his hands on a few sick people and heal them. He was amazed at their lack of faith" (Mark 6:5–6).

Father Damien

JANUARY 21

Tourists visit the Hawaiian Island of Molokai to enjoy the beaches and charm. But Father Damien came for a different reason. He came to help people die. You see, lepers came there first, starting in about 1840. They lived in isolation on a tract of land set aside just for them.

When Father Damien heard of their plight, he begged his supervisors to let him move to Molokai to live with the lepers. The year was 1873. He said, "I make myself a leper with the lepers to gain all to Jesus Christ."

Father Damien entered the world of the lepers. He dressed their sores, hugged their children, and buried their dead. Eventually, he would contract their disease. On April 15, 1889, Father Damien died of leprosy.

Father Damien did for the Molokai lepers what Jesus did for each of us. Not content to simply "treat" mankind, Jesus became a man. He joined the human race. The Bible says, "For this reason he had to be made like them, fully human in every way, in order that he might become a merciful and faithful high priest in service to God, and that he might make atonement for the sins of the people" (Heb. 2:17).

Recovery Step: Recognize that you are not alone. Embrace the one who understands every temptation you will ever face because he's been there. In fact, he still is.

The Fence

JANUARY 22

There was a young boy who struggled with profanity. His father took him to a field across the street from their home where there was an old fence. He gave his son a box of nails and a hammer, and said, "Every time you say a bad word, hammer a new nail into the fence."

Each day, the boy went to the fence and hammered in his nails. Eventually, he began to turn things around, cussing less each day. One day, he went to his dad, full of joy. "Dad, I've quit cussing! I'm no longer having to hammer nails into the fence."

With that, his dad took the boy to the fence with a new set of instructions. "Each day you don't cuss, remove one nail from the fence."

Months later, the boy proudly removed his last nail and brought that nail to his dad. "I'm so glad there are no more nails," said the father. "But notice that the holes from those nails are still there."

His lesson was that the angry words of his son still had lasting effects, long after he turned things around. For our purposes, let's substitute your addictive behaviors for the profanity in this story.

Years after you quit acting out, the pain you inflicted on those closest to you has left scars that live on for years.

Recovery Step: Actions have consequences. "A man reaps what he sows" (Gal. 6:7). It's good to remove the nails. But it's better to have never hammered them into your fence in the first place.

The Circus Is Still Here

JANUARY 23

An interesting study was conducted that revealed the degree to which most of us overestimate our own abilities. Participants were given a series of words to spell. After the test, each person was asked how many words they thought they had spelled correctly. Several participants said they thought they had gotten 100 percent of the words right. But on average, they had only gotten 80 percent of the words right.

A similar test was given with true-false answers. Of those who thought they had gotten every question right, they were again on average only right 80 percent of the time.

In recovery, we make a little progress and then overestimate how far we have come. George Carlin said it as only he could: "Just because you got the monkey off your back doesn't mean the circus has left town."

If you have achieved a few months of sobriety, if you are no longer viewing porn, if masturbation is in your past, congratulations! You have gotten the monkey off your back. But that doesn't mean the circus has left town. There is still much work to be done.

Recovery Step: "Pray that you will not fall into temptation" (Luke 22:40).

Group

JANUARY 24

God never intended us to do life alone. This thing called "connection" is magic. You can't find recovery without it. Isolation is not your friend. Community is your friend.

Paul told the church, "Encourage one another and build each other up" (1 Thess. 5:11).

Dr. Nathan Heflick is the senior lecturer at the University of Lincoln in the United Kingdom. He writes extensively on what he calls "the emphatic appeal of being in a group." He found that almost any shared characteristic can lead us to form lasting, intimate bonds within a group.

Recovery Step: Perhaps the missing ingredient to your recovery is a group. Dr. Brené Brown says this connection produces the energy necessary for self-improvement. Go all in with a group this week.

Just Whistle

JANUARY 25

Writer David Redding told of his days growing up on a farm in Scotland. As a young boy, he was given a beautiful black puppy that he named Teddy. Redding and Teddy were inseparable. When Redding had to go off to war, he was unable to return for more than two years. But when he got within a half mile of the family farm, he heard Teddy barking.

Redding whistled, and Teddy recognized that whistle and came bounding toward him. Redding observed, "If a dog can receive me back after I've been away for such a long time, how much more will God welcome and receive me when I return to him."

Perhaps you have wandered off, run off, or veered off the right path—away from God and recovery. Just whistle. Let God hear your voice. He will recognize you and welcome you back.

Recovery Step: "Return to the Lord your God, for he is gracious and compassionate, slow to anger and abounding in love" (Joel 2:13).

Off the Cliff

JANUARY 26

John Bevere has produced the best YouTube video on addiction recovery I have seen. Look it up. It's called *Killing Kryptonite*. In the video a blind man is slowly walking toward a cliff and an inevitable death. His only hope is two men who see him. They debate whether they should risk offending the man by telling him how to walk or to "love" him with only words of affirmation. At the end they decide to "love" him—as he disappears off the edge.

James admonishes his readers, "My brothers and sisters, if one of you should wander from the truth and someone should bring that person back, remember this: Whoever turns a sinner from the error of their way will save them from death and cover over a multitude of sins" (James 5:19–20).

We all know people who are headed over the edge. And God has strategically placed us in their path. Their hope is us. Let me say that again—their hope is us.

Who do you know who is struggling with addiction? More importantly, what are you doing about it?

When you help others, you help yourself. So ask God to lead you to the person you can lead to him.

Recovery Step: Help someone who is struggling today. In the process, you will help yourself.

Box of Chocolates

JANUARY 27

Life is unpredictable. Don't take my word for it. Solomon said, "At best, life is unpredictable" (Eccles. 9:7 VOICE).

The great philosopher Forrest Gump said it in a way we can all understand. "My mama always said life was like a box of chocolates. You never know what you're gonna get."

You know something else that is a box of chocolates?

Recovery.

There are days filled with dark caramels (yum!). Other days, you bite into a piece of coconut dressed up like pure chocolate (yuk!). The answer, George Patton said, was to "prepare for the unknown." Prepare for the next trigger, test, and temptation. Prepare for what might be around the next turn. Not every turn in the road is lined with demons, but some are.

The answer is to prepare, stay sober, and keep working your program. That way, when you bite into a hunk of coconut, you'll be ready.

Recovery Step: Do the work on the front end so when your temptation comes, you'll be ready.

Chocolate Chip Study

JANUARY 28

In 1998, Case Western Reserve University conducted an interesting study on self-control. Participants were surrounded by fresh chocolate chip cookies but were told to resist the temptation and eat radishes instead. While they followed this directive, it took a toll. As their activities were monitored in the following hours, it was found that they lacked focus, and their capacity to function and make wise decisions was diminished for a few hours.

Dr. Roy Baumeister, who directed the research, concluded, "Self-control gets used up and needs time to be replenished before you use it again."

That's the thing about self-control. It always gets used up. That's why every addict fails in his own strength. And that is where the supernatural power of God enters the picture.

Paul wrote, "The fruit of the Spirit is love, joy, peace, forbearance, kindness, goodness, faithfulness, gentleness, and self-control" (Gal. 5:22–23).

Recovery Step: When temptation hits, practice self-control. And if you are in short supply, seek the filling and power of the Holy Spirit.

Cooking with Wine

JANUARY 29

We are always looking for something to soothe our pain. That's why I often say that addiction isn't a bad problem as much as it is a bad solution. We use it to make something else go away, if just for the moment. Addiction is just one drug that does the trick.

W. C. Fields said, "I always cook with wine. Sometimes I even add it to the food."

The prophet Isaiah seemed to have a good understanding of the human dilemma. He asked, "Why spend money on what is not bread, and your labor on what does not satisfy?" (Isa. 55:2).

What are you turning to in order to soothe your pain? The next time you turn to your drug of choice, just remember, the solution is worse than the problem. And then the solution becomes the problem.

> **Recovery Step:** The next time you feel driven to soothe your pain, make sure the cure isn't worse than the problem.

Never Forget

JANUARY 30

Jim Valvano's story has inspired a generation. I still remember that awful night in Albuquerque, New Mexico. The date was April 4, 1983. North Carolina State, coached by Valvano, beat my beloved Houston Cougars for the NCAA men's basketball championship. Valvano proceeded to run all over the court looking for someone to hug. It was one of the great upsets in sports history.

Ten years later, almost to the date, Valvano lost a courageous battle with cancer at the age of 47. But it was his battle with cancer, not his success on the court, that touched millions.

Treasuring every day and knowing his fate, Coach Valvano said, "I will thank God for the day and the moment I have."

What Jim Valvano did, we all must do. Never forget your blessings, and never take today's moments for granted.

"But when the kindness and love of God our Savior appeared, he saved us, not because of righteous things we had done, but because of his mercy. He saved us through the washing of rebirth and renewal by the Holy Spirit" (Titus 3:4–5).

Recovery Step: Take a moment to thank God for the blessings of your past and commit this day to him—not next week or next year, just today.

Chocolate Easter Bunnies

JANUARY 31

When I was a child, Easter was a fun time. Mom and Dad hid Easter eggs all over the house and yard. My brother and I filled our baskets with all kinds of calories and fat grams.

But the prize was the coveted chocolate Easter bunny. I begged for one every year. Mom usually gave in, and on Easter I was allowed to eat it. I started with an ear. But with the first bite came a disappointment that I remember to this day. You see, the ear was hollow. In fact, the whole Easter bunny was hollow. What looked like 5 pounds of pure chocolate was mostly just air. It looked great, smelled great, and always drew me in. But each bite left me wanting more.

The Easter bunny is a picture of addiction. The lure is compelling. But what looks fulfilling always leaves us hollow. The bite never matches the look.

Your "Easter bunny" will never completely satisfy. You have two options: Give up your hollow bunny or keep eating more bunnies in hopes they will eventually satisfy.

Spoiler alert: They never will.

Recovery Step: "Taste and see that the Lord is good; blessed is the one who takes refuge in him" (Ps. 34:8).

FEBRUARY

You can't go back and change the beginning
but you can start where you are and change the ending.

—C. S. Lewis

The Real Thing

FEBRUARY 1

One day, Charlie Brown lamented, "Someday, we will all die, Snoopy." Snoopy replied, "True, but on all the other days, we will not."

If you are among the readers who are alive today, you need to define what it means to really live. Let me help you with that. To live is to love others—really love others.

The Bible says it like this: "Don't just pretend to love others. Really love them" (Rom. 12:9 NLT).

The problem is that rather than love people, we use people. And usually we don't even see it—especially in our addiction.

Saint Augustine described the love we are to express for one another. "What does love look like? It has the hands to help others. It has the feet to hasten to the poor and needy. It has eyes to see misery and want. It has the ears to hear the sighs and sorrows of men. That is what love looks like."

Recovery Step: Saint Augustine was right. Love has the hands to help others. So get after it. As God brings someone in need into your life, love them. Really love them.

The Power of Forgiveness

FEBRUARY 2

The power of forgiveness is well-documented.

Johns Hopkins Medicine conducted studies that conclude that our health is greatly impacted by our willingness to forgive those who have harmed us. Their findings: "Studies have found that the act of forgiveness can reap huge rewards for your health, lowering the risk of heart attack; improving cholesterol levels and sleep; and reducing pain, blood pressure, and levels of anxiety, depression and stress."

Paul said it like this: "Be kind and compassionate to one another, forgiving each other, just as in Christ God forgave you" (Eph. 4:32).

I'm guessing you didn't wake up one day and say, "I think I'll become an addict." Much of who you are is the result of the actions of others. But the next move is yours. Forgiveness does not come easily, but it beats the alternative.

Recovery Step: Dr. Karen Swartz wrote, "There is an enormous physical burden to being hurt and disappointed." That burden is not fair to you. But to not forgive the offending party will only make matters worse. You deserve better.

Storming the Court

FEBRUARY 3

It finally happened. On February 14, 2024, the Detroit Mercy college men's basketball team won a game. Their record twenty-seven-game losing streak had come to an end. With a win over IUPUI, the Titans notched their first win of the season on their home court. The fan went nuts.

Yes, the fan—not the "fans."

A lone fan stormed the court, dancing around like his team had just won the National Championship. He jumped, hollered, and celebrated, running around like he was on fire. There were other fans in the arena, but this guy was the only one to run out onto the court.

Sometimes we need to celebrate, even if no one else does.

The Bible has this promise: "So do not fear, for I am with you; do not be dismayed, for I am your God. I will strengthen you and help you; I will uphold you with my righteous right hand" (Isa. 41:10).

If you feel like you're on an island, it's okay. If you are the only one who storms the court, that's fine. God gets it.

Recovery Step: Learn to storm the court when no one else does.

Bottoms Up

FEBRUARY 4

Every person I've seen get well had one thing in common. They all hit bottom.

The Old Testament tells the story of such a woman. When a widow was out of food and had become desperate, she cried out to Elisha for help. Without her husband to provide for her, the widow feared she would lose her sons to slavery. She needed to provide for them immediately, but she had precious few resources, and her family was hungry. Elisha asked her what she had in the house.

The widow had only a little oil. "She went and told the man of God, and he said, 'Go, sell the oil and pay your debts. You and your sons can live on what is left'" (2 Kings 4:7). In obedience, she started to fill the jars with oil, and God miraculously multiplied the oil.

The woman shifted her focus from what she had lost to what she had left. And then the blessings began to flow.

F. B. Meyer said, "We must get to the end of ourselves before God can begin in us." Teddy Roosevelt said it like this: "When you reach the end of your rope, tie a knot and hang on."

Recovery Step: If you are to the end of your rope, if you are truly desperate, you are in a good place. Why? Because it is only when you let go that God takes over.

Room with a View

FEBRUARY 5

In a 1984 study of twenty-three surgical patients, cited by Dr. Roger Ulrich with Chalmers University of Technology, it was found that hospital patients whose rooms had a window view recovered more quickly than patients whose rooms had no views. Consequently, they spent less time in the hospital. The conclusion was that when we are constantly given a view of hope, we recover more quickly.

God has given each of us incredible views. And you don't have to go far to see them. Pastor and author Mark Batterson advocates for "two-foot field trips." By that, he means that we are surrounded with God's creation and his creativity. There are views to behold on every side.

Here's some good advice, all the way from the oldest book in the Bible: "Listen to this, Job; stop and consider God's wonders. Do you know how God controls the clouds and makes his lightning flash?" (Job 37:14–15).

Recovery Step: You don't need to go to the Swiss Alps or the Islands of the Bahamas to see the wonders of God. Just take a two-foot field trip. Just look outside.

Rubik's Cube

FEBRUARY 6

Guess who created the Rubik's Cube?

Charlie Cube.

Erno Rubik.

Here's a better question. How long did it take Erno Rubik to solve the cube after he created it?

Answer: one month.

The current world record is 4.22 seconds.

Here's what happened. Erno Rubik invented the famous cube, but it took someone else to learn how to solve it quickly.

Lesson: We all have our strengths.

What are you good at? I suggest that whatever that is, God wants to use that gift to somehow help others who are also in recovery. God never endows us with gifts, strengths, or talents that he does not want us to use.

"Each of you should use whatever gift you have received to serve others, as faithful stewards of God's grace in its various forms" (1 Pet. 4:10).

Recovery Step: Use one of your strengths to help someone else this week.

Breaking Free

FEBRUARY 7

A mailman with a new route came to a house with a mean-looking dog on the porch. When the man approached the mailbox, the dog jumped 20 feet in the air and then sat down. The owner walked out to check on the commotion.

The mailman asked the resident, "Why did your dog do that?"

The owner replied, "We removed his chain yesterday, but he doesn't realize it."

Like many of us, the dog was living in the past. He assumed that yesterday's chains still had him bound today. The mailman triggered his reaction. He jumped and barked but then acted like he was still chained to his past.

Freedom from your addiction is a daily choice. Yesterday's chains do not bind you today; only today's choices can do that. Like the dog, you will be triggered sometime today. That is not a choice. But how you respond is a choice.

The Bible tells the story of a man bound by chains. When he was set free, for the first time in his life he was found "in his right mind" (Mark 5:15). Sobriety does that. It puts us in our right minds.

Recovery Step: Pray for power to overcome your triggers today. Then claim the freedom God promises those who truly seek him.

Learn from Leonardo

FEBRUARY 8

Do you tend to be too hard on yourself? Meet the president of the Too Hard on Myself Club. Perhaps you've heard of him.

Leonardo da Vinci.

Noted as perhaps the most accomplished artist in history, da Vinci is credited with the *Mona Lisa* and the *Last Supper*, two of the most revered paintings ever.

But da Vinci didn't see himself as others did. In 1519, he said, "I have offended God and mankind because my work did not reach the quality it should have."

And then he died.

Paul said, "Run your best in the race of faith" (1 Tim. 6:12 GNT).

Once we do that, the rest is in God's hands. I'm sure you've felt just like Leonardo. You have failed to be all you wish you could be. So you missed your goal of perfection. Now you need to settle for progress, which should have been your goal all along.

Recovery Step: Accept your failures and past. Do the next best thing. Strive for progress, not perfection.

Tree Bark

FEBRUARY 9

In 2009, a dendrologist named Dr. Martin Gossner was researching the resilience of tree bark. When he cut back a piece of bark on an old tree in the Bavarian Forest National Park, he was stunned by his discovery of the living organisms behind that piece of bark:

- 2,042 insects and other organisms
- 257 various species

The tree, Dr. Gossner concluded, had become its own ecosystem.

If you ever doubt the complexity of God and his creation, cut a piece of bark. Or better yet, seek God on behalf of your recovery. In him, you will find a Creator who knows you intimately and whose healing powers run far deeper than you can imagine.

Recovery Step: "The heavens declare the glory of God; the skies proclaim the work of his hands" (Ps. 19:1). The God of the universe stands ready to partner with you in your recovery. There is no need to go it alone.

The Key to Success

FEBRUARY 10

If you want to know where you will be in five years, take a look right now at the habits you practice every day. Blaise Pascal said, "The strength of a man's virtue should not be measured by his special exertions, but by his habitual acts."

An extensive research project surveyed some of the world's most successful men and women from the world of sports, entertainment, politics, and business. They asked each person to identify the thing that contributed most to their success from among four choices. These were the results:

- Luck: 6 percent
- Talent: 19 percent
- Good decisions: 25 percent
- Consistent habits: 50 percent

Paul said it like this: "Therefore, my beloved brothers, be steadfast, immovable, always abounding in the work of the Lord" (1 Cor. 15:58 ESV).

Recovery Step: If you want to attain highly successful recovery, you need to establish some consistent habits—and then stick to them. Make a habit of doing recovery work every day.

Desperation

FEBRUARY 11

Desperate times call for desperate measures. Desperation is the birthplace of recovery. You will never find lasting, sustainable recovery without it. You have to want recovery more than anything else.

I can't think of a more desperate situation in the Bible than that of Lazarus. The man was dying, so his sisters came to Jesus and pleaded for him to heal their brother. Jesus responded, "This sickness will not end in death" (John 11:4). And then two days later, Lazarus died.

So what gives?

Notice what Jesus did not say. He didn't say Lazarus wouldn't die. He said the sickness would not end in death.

Think about it. If Jesus had healed Lazarus before he died, he would have just been another nameless guy in the Bible. What made Lazarus famous was not his healing but his resurrection.

God is the master of resurrection. Think about your own recovery. Your addiction may have killed your marriage, your job, your finances, and your self-esteem. But God's promise is that it won't end there. God always gets the final word.

Recovery Step: Become desperate for recovery as you've never been desperate for anything else in your life.

Name This Guy

FEBRUARY 12

Can you name this person?

Born in Mississippi, he was raised in rooming houses. He wanted to be a musician but never had any kind of formal musical training. When he tried out for choir in the eighth grade, his music teacher gave him a C. Undeterred, he bought his first guitar the next day. He was told he had no talent, but he refused to give up on his dreams.

His name? Elvis Presley.

Elvis would go on to sell more albums than any solo artist who has ever lived.

The Bible offers this simple advice to all who have big dreams: "Be all the more diligent" (2 Pet. 1:10 ESV).

The difference between failure and success is often just that—diligence. That is especially true of recovery. Staying at the task when you really want to quit will make all the difference.

> **Recovery Step:** Get on a daily recovery plan. Then stick to it.

Honus Wagner Card

FEBRUARY 13

Did you collect baseball cards as a kid? Are those cards boxed up in the attic? After reading this, you might want to take another look at those cards. One particular card could change your life.

The T206 Honus Wagner card is considered the most valuable card ever produced, drawing as much as $10 million per card. It was initially designed and issued by the American Tobacco Company. Wagner refused to allow production because he didn't want children to buy cigarette packs to get his card. As a result, less than ten cards exist today, and each is worth a fortune.

Honus Wagner is to be congratulated for taking a stand against tobacco at a time when few others did. He exemplified Proverbs 10:9: "Whoever walks in integrity walks securely, but whoever takes crooked paths will be found out."

Let me ask you three questions.

1. What are you willing to do to take a stand?
2. Are you willing to be mocked because of your faith?
3. Do you value your sobriety when no one else does?

Recovery Step: Do the right thing whether others do or not.

The Four-Letter Word for Recovery

FEBRUARY 14

There is a four-letter word for recovery: *rest.* It is not an option. It's in the Ten Commandments. "Six days you shall labor and do all your work, but the seventh day is a sabbath to the Lord your God" (Exod. 20:9–10).

The National Sleep Foundation says we need seven to nine hours of sleep every day. The National Institute for Occupational Safety and Health has found twelve benefits to a day of rest. The first is that it reduces stress. And nothing triggers addiction like stress.

I suggest you go a step further. Some of the best advice my sponsor ever gave me was to have a Recovery Day every month or so. A Recovery Day is a day of rest. It includes solitude, reading recovery material, meditation, and prayer.

William Wordsworth wrote, "Rest and be thankful." Embrace rest. It's God's four-letter word for recovery. Every seven days you need a day of rest. Your recovery depends on it.

Recovery Step: Plan a day of rest this week. And plan a Recovery Day this month. Mark both dates on your calendar and make them a priority.

Eighth Wonder of the World

FEBRUARY 15

There have been a lot of definitions of the eighth wonder of the world that have floated around over the years. Albert Einstein called the eighth wonder of the world—ready for this?—compound interest.

We overestimate what we can accomplish in a day, but we underestimate what God can do in a year or two—or ten.

Consistency beats intensity every time. Give it enough time and you can transform your body, your mind, your marriage, your finances, your attitude.

And your recovery.

Maybe that's what Paul had in mind when he wrote, "Therefore, my beloved brothers, be steadfast, immovable, always abounding in the work of the Lord" (1 Cor. 15:58 ESV).

Recovery Step: Identify one simple thing you can do in the area of recovery. Then do it every day.

Four Days

FEBRUARY 16

Day 1: A man walked down a street and fell in a hole.

Day 2: The man walked down the street, saw the hole, but slipped into the hole.

Day 3: The man walked down the street, tried to avoid the hole, but was bumped by someone else and stumbled into the hole.

Day 4: The man picked a different street.

Jesus addressed this topic when he said, "Enter through the narrow gate. For wide is the gate and broad is the road that leads to destruction, and many enter through it. But small is the gate and narrow the road that leads to life, and only a few find it." (Matt. 7:13–14).

Here's the lesson. Rather than trying to avoid the hole, avoid the road altogether.

Recovery Step: In order to avoid the hole of relapse, pick a new route.

The Silver Bullet

FEBRUARY 17

Is there a silver bullet to sobriety? Is there one key, one thing that will bring recovery? Is there a simple fix?

The answer is yes, but you aren't going to like what it is. It's called discipline.

Paul told young Timothy how to win in life. "Fight the good fight of the faith" (1 Tim. 6:12).

I've seen boxers fight, and I've seen them train. The fight is determined by the training. It is the miles of roadwork and hundreds of rounds in the gym that create the successful fighter. It is what is done when no one is watching that makes the fighter great.

In your addiction, you have found your strongest opponent. He will come at you with everything he's got. And he keeps getting up, no matter how many rounds you have won. He is relentless in his attack and unyielding in his efforts. And even though you may be ahead on points, he can still take you out with a single punch in the final round unless you are diligent in your preparation and disciplined in your defense. Jim Rohn was right: "Discipline is the bridge between goals and accomplishment."

Recovery Step: If you are committed to your sobriety, you must embrace the discipline that precedes each battle—discipline to go to meetings, make calls, and never give up.

Just One Step

FEBRUARY 18

God made the mustard seed, and he knows how to use it.

Mustard seeds aren't that impressive. They are just 0.1 inch in diameter. But mustard trees can reach heights of 30 feet with branches 20 feet long.

You know the verse: "If you have faith as small as a mustard seed, you can say to this mountain, 'Move from here to there,' and it will move. Nothing will be impossible for you" (Matt. 17:20–21).

Here's what I've learned about faith. What matters is not the size of our faith but the object of our faith.

In recovery, we must turn to the One who can do for us what we cannot do for ourselves. God won't do recovery without me. And I can't do recovery without him. That doesn't require any big steps, just small steps in the right direction.

Recovery Step: Take one step in the right direction today.

Chess Boxing

FEBRUARY 19

I play chess. My son boxes. In fact, he boxes better than I play chess. In Finland, you can do both—at the same time.

It's called "chess boxing."

Players make a few chess moves and then engage in a round of boxing. They keep alternating between chess and boxing until they've played eleven alternating rounds. It's the ultimate bout of brain and brawn.

It's important to know the rules; otherwise, you might sit down to a friendly game of chess, and after you move your rook, your opponent gives you an unexpected uppercut to the jaw.

Yep, you need to know the rules. Maybe Paul was a chess boxer. We don't know. The Bible is silent on the subject. But he sure sounded like one when he said, "An athlete is not crowned unless he competes according to the rules" (2 Tim. 2:5 ESV).

There's this other game called recovery. You can win, but only if you know the rules—stay desperate, surrender to God, walk in community.

Recovery Step: Commit to the rules of recovery. That's the only way you'll win.

The Untold Price We Pay

FEBRUARY 20

The Bible tells the story of a man named Amnon who fell in love with Tamar, his half-sister (2 Sam. 13). Here we find the progressive nature of addiction. What Amnon took in with his eyes became lust. Lust led to fantasy, which resulted in acting out.

Then we discover the final chapter in every episode of acting out. Amnon's brief moment of ecstasy was followed by an overwhelming sense of shame. What happened in Amnon's life is the story of every addict. Amnon wanted what he shouldn't have and didn't want it once he had it.

Immediately after he committed his sin, "Then suddenly Amnon's love turned to hate, and he hated her even more than he had loved her" (2 Sam. 13:15 NLT). Amnon became a permanent wreck, and he discovered a hard truth: The one thing more painful than not feeding our lust is feeding our lust.

The next time you fantasize about crossing the boundaries God has put in place, pause just long enough to play out the end of the story in your head. It never ends well.

When you do cross those lines, even if just in your head, keep the words of Watchman Nee close by: "Now is the hour we should humbly prostrate ourselves before God, willing to be convinced afresh of our sins by the Holy Spirit."

Recovery Step: When you are drawn toward lust in your heart, remind yourself how the story always ends.

Six Hundred People Are Watching You

FEBRUARY 21

According to research conducted by Columbia University, you probably know about 600 people. That means 600 people are watching you. To each of them, you make a difference—good or bad.

Now I'm not saying you know 600 people well, just that you know 600 people. The question is, what difference does your life make to each of them?

Thomas Jefferson said, "Whenever you do a thing, act as if all the world were watching."

Jesus said it even better. "Let your light shine before others, so that they may see your good deeds and glorify your Father in heaven" (Matt. 5:16).

Whether you are an addict or have been traumatized by one, someone is watching. What you do next—starting today—will make a difference, not only in your life but in the lives of others.

Recovery Step: You are being watched by 600 people. Live the life today that will impact your world tomorrow.

Pushing Trains

FEBRUARY 22

Do you ever tire of straining to stay sober, of trying to do the right thing? Perhaps you can relate to the rural pastor.

The pastor was spotted sitting by the train track each morning. A church member asked him what he was doing. "Why do you sit here watching the train go by each day?" she asked him.

"It's simple," replied the pastor. "I enjoy watching something move that I don't have to push."

Life is most effective when we leave the pushing to God. The psalmist wrote, "The Lord is my strength and my shield; my heart trusts in him, and he helps me. My heart leaps for joy, and with my song I praise him" (Ps. 28:7).

J. I. Packer said it well with these now-famous words: "Our high and privileged calling is to do the will of God in the power of God for the glory of God."

It is natural to want to do all the pushing ourselves. But it doesn't work. We need to learn to let go and let the Conductor take over.

Recovery Step: Quit pushing. Relax. Turn control of your train—and your life—over to God.

Unmasked

FEBRUARY 23

Do you remember this verse from the New Testament? "And we all, who with unveiled faces contemplate the Lord's glory, are being transformed into his image with ever-increasing glory, which comes from the Lord, who is the Spirit" (2 Cor. 3:18).

That's powerful! Did you catch the two words that tell us the requirement for being truly transformed by God?

Unveiled face.

We must remove the mask and be willing to be known. And that, my friend, is as scary as meatloaf at the local diner.

But it's true—and necessary. I read this in my daily devotion the other day: "The greatest characteristic a Christian can exhibit is this completely unveiled openness before God" (Oswald Chambers).

Recovery Step: John Piper wrote, "There is always one person you must relate to who knows everything about you." That's true. But why don't you start by taking your mask off before God?

Patting Birds

FEBRUARY 24

Linus of "Peanuts" fame was taking a lot of heat because of his newly found "calling." He liked to pat birds on their heads. Distressed little birds would approach him, lower their feathered pates to be patted, sigh deeply, and then walk away satisfied. That brought Linus indescribable joy.

Charlie Brown and Lucy asked him why he was doing that.

"What's wrong with patting birds on their heads?" Linus asked.

"Are you kidding me?" Charlie Brown asked. "What's wrong with it is that nobody else is doing it!"

Joshua was willing to stand up for God even when no one else was doing it. "But if serving the Lord seems undesirable to you, then choose for yourselves this day whom you will serve. . . . But as for me and my household, we will serve the Lord" (Josh. 24:15).

If you are going to overcome your addiction, you need to take the steps of recovery, even if nobody else is doing it.

Recovery Step: Take the steps of recovery, whether anyone else does or not.

Lightning and Giraffes

FEBRUARY 25

Let's talk lightning and giraffes.

We'll start with lightning. There are 1.4 billion lightning strikes per year around the globe, which is forty-four strikes per second. Lightning hits 270 people per year, and about 10 percent of those unfortunates die as a result.

But the news is even worse for giraffes.

From 1996 to 2020, studies compared the frequency of lightning strikes for people versus giraffes, taking into account the size of their population. This is what was found. Giraffes are thirty times more likely to get hit by lightning than their human counterparts.

Giraffes need to keep their heads down.

That's actually good advice for all of us. The Bible says, "Let your eyes look straight ahead; fix your gaze directly before you" (Prov. 4:25).

Recovery Step: Don't look back. Look ahead. Keep your eyes on Jesus.

Share a Glove

FEBRUARY 26

The story is told of a man walking down the street on a very cold day in a poor part of town. He saw two boys playing, and neither of them had gloves. So the man removed his wool gloves and walked over and handed them to one of the boys. Almost immediately, that boy handed one of the gloves to the other boy.

That is the picture of Step 12—helping others—of the 12-Step Program used largely by Alcoholics Anonymous. Step 12 should be carried out organically with little thought. If you are committed to sharing your gloves with another person in need, God will bring that person across your path. I guarantee it.

Don't hold back. The Bible says, "Remember this: Whoever sows sparingly will also reap sparingly, and whoever sows generously will also reap generously" (2 Cor. 9:6).

We live in a really cold world. Look around. Find someone who needs a glove.

Recovery Step: Do two things today. First, ask God to direct you to a person you can help in their recovery. Second, do it!

7th Step Prayer

FEBRUARY 27

Paul wasn't talking about recovery, but he could have been when he said, "It does not, therefore, depend on human desire or effort, but on God's mercy" (Rom. 9:16).

Saint Augustine said, "Trust the past to God's mercy, the present to God's love, and the future to God's providence."

You have trusted your own instincts, wisdom, and best efforts for too long. I invite you to join me in saying the 7th Step Prayer today:

> My Creator, I am now willing that you should have all of me, good and bad. I pray now that you remove from me every single defect of character that stands in the way of my usefulness to you and to others. Grant me strength, as I go out from here, to do your will.

Recovery Step: I pray that prayer every morning before I start my day. It has served me well as I seek to walk in daily surrender. I encourage you to make that part of your daily recovery routine as well.

Did Jesus Really Say That?

FEBRUARY 28

Jesus came upon a man who had been sick for thirty-eight years. We can assume the man had tried everything—doctors, religion, and home remedies. Still he was sick. He had played his last card. He was out of options. So he looked to Jesus.

And Jesus asked him the strangest question: "Do you want to get well?" (John 5:6). Was that a serious question? Sure, he wanted to get well! Who wouldn't?

But Jesus's question really wasn't one of desire but of desperation. "Do you [really] want to get well?" He told the man, who could not walk, to pick up his mat and walk. That required a willingness to look the part of a fool. What if the healing didn't really take place?

When the man did the improbable, Jesus did the impossible. And the man was healed.

The first key to freedom is desperation. Most of us are more comfortable with old problems than new solutions. So we never find freedom.

Real freedom comes when we are more desperate for God than his blessings.

Recovery Step: Seek God with a desperate heart.

Froot Loops

FEBRUARY 29

Let's start the day with a deep philosophical question.

Did you know that even though Froot Loops are many colors, they all have the same flavor?

While you ponder that, let me move on. The Bible says, "Just as a body, though one, has many parts, but all its many parts form one body, so it is with Christ" (1 Cor. 12:12).

People are like Froot Loops. We are all a bit fruity, and we all look different from one another. And that's good. Who would ever buy a box of Froot Loops if they announced that from now on, each Froot Loop will look the same as all the rest?

Let's celebrate our differences. In recovery, some people place more emphasis on going to meetings. For others, it's all about making a zillion calls a day. Some live for a daily podcast. Of course, most people in recovery count the days until my newest book comes out.

We are all Froot Loops on some level—similar to each other but different. And that's okay.

Recovery Step: Be the Froot Loop that God created you to be while enjoying the other Froot Loops that God has placed in your box.

MARCH

God is ready to assume full responsibility
for the life wholly yielded to Him.

—Andrew Murray

Lighthouse Keepers

MARCH 1

A few years ago, Beth and I vacationed in northern Minnesota where the views of Lake Superior are simply stunning. I return every year on a personal writing retreat. It is a highlight of my year.

One of the sites to not miss is the Split Rock Lighthouse that overlooks the massive lake. While touring the lighthouse, I learned something I didn't know about lighthouses and lighthouse keepers.

The most important job of a lighthouse keeper is to clean the lens.

The same could be said for each of us. Paul talked about seeing through a glass "dimly" (1 Cor. 13:12 ESV).

One of the tasks of recovery is to see ourselves clearly. Thomas Carlyle said, "Our main business is not to see what lies dimly at a distance, but to do what lies clearly at hand."

Recovery Step: Take a closer look at yourself—your sobriety, fantasy life, habits, and spiritual disciplines. Don't focus too much on what lies in the distance. Look at what is right in front of you. But first, ask God to clean your lens.

PPA

MARCH 2

I am a card-carrying member of PPA—People Pleasers Anonymous. I suspect most of us are. And making others happy is generally a good thing, up to a point. But as addicts, we can cross that point almost without notice.

Norman Vincent Peale said, "The trouble with most of us is that we'd rather be ruined by praise than saved by criticism."

Sometimes we have to make a choice. Sometimes we have to make decisions that feed our recovery rather than the expectations of others. Sometimes we have to do things that deepen our personal faith and sobriety, even when others don't get it. And sometimes others won't like us for that.

And we have to be okay with that.

Recovery Step: Consider the following question posed by the Apostle Paul: "Am I now trying to win the approval of human beings, or of God? Or am I trying to please people? If I were still trying to please people, I would not be a servant of Christ" (Gal. 1:10).

Can My Addiction Go Away?

MARCH 3

I get this question a lot: "Can God remove my addiction?" Or said another way, "Can I be completely healed of my addiction?"

The short answer is yes. Of course God can remove any addiction 100 percent.

"This is what the Lord, the God of your father David, says: 'I have heard your prayer and seen your tears; I will heal you'" (2 Kings 20:5).

God can completely heal your addiction because he is God. He can also regrow an arm that is lost in an accident, remove Stage 4 cancer, and restore sight to the blind.

But don't put God in a box. He is not a genie awaiting your next command.

I have observed that for every 100 men who pray for their addiction to be taken away, maybe one sees it happen. Why is that? The reason addiction rarely just goes away is that the causes don't go away. Addiction is the result of trauma, abuse, and isolation. Those bring lasting scars, and scars have consequences.

Recovery Step: Can God remove your addiction? Sure, he can. But in his sovereign grace, he may not.

Terry Bradshaw

MARCH 4

Hall-of-Fame coach Chuck Noll won 68 percent of his NFL games, with Terry Bradshaw as his quarterback. When anyone else played quarterback, Noll only won 47 percent of his games. With Tom Brady at quarterback, Bill Belichick won 77 percent of the time; with other quarterbacks, he won just 48 percent. And Marv Levy won 66 percent of the time, as long as Jim Kelly was quarterback. When anyone else was playing quarterback, Levy won just 42 percent of his games.

It doesn't matter how great you are; you can't win by yourself—in football, in life, or in recovery. Just as Moses needed Aaron, David needed Jonathan, and Paul needed Timothy, you need someone to walk with you through the journey ahead.

Psalm 133:1 reads, "How good and pleasant it is when God's people live together in unity!" We all need each other at one time or another.

Recovery Step: You need this person—an accountability partner, fellow climber, sponsor, or friend. Recovery is a team sport. You can win, but you can't do it by yourself.

Pitcairn Island

MARCH 5

Pitcairn Island is one of the most remote places on earth. Set in the Pacific Ocean, it is home to just fifty residents, and for good reason. You can only get there if you fly to Tahiti and then sail for 1,200 miles. Then you transfer to a ruby dinghy, take your climbing gear, and eventually scale the 900-foot rock cliffs to the tiny village.

Pitcairn Island is a metaphor for loneliness and isolation. Pitcairn Island is a metaphor for addiction.

Solomon wrote, "Whoever isolates himself seeks his own desire; he breaks out against all sound judgment" (Prov. 18:1 ESV).

Here are the facts: Nobody has it made, we're all afraid, we don't want to be alone, and we've all got to have a home.

Recovery Step: Join a group. Get in a church. Make some new friends. That is the key to sanity, hope, and freedom.

Missing Shovel

MARCH 6

In a concentration camp, a guard announced that a shovel was missing. Screaming at the men, he kept insisting someone had stolen it. He shouldered his rifle, ready to kill one prisoner at a time until a confession was made.

As the story continues, a Scottish soldier broke ranks, stood stiffly at attention, and said, "I did it." The guard killed the man. As they returned to camp, the shovels were counted. The guard had made a mistake. No shovel was missing after all.

Who does that? What kind of person would take the blame for something he didn't do? When you find the adjective, attach it to Jesus. Isaiah 53:6 (MSG) says, "God has piled all our sins, everything we've done wrong on him." Christ lived the life we could not live and took the punishment we could not take to offer the hope we cannot resist.

Recovery Step: Let Jesus do what he came to do. Give him your shame, your guilt, your addiction, your everything.

Dwell in Possibility

MARCH 7

By all accounts, Emily Dickinson was a recluse. The famous poet rarely left home. She maintained her few friendships by writing and sending cards. Still, she found a way to make a difference.

Emily Dickinson left her mark—1,800 poems. Among those poems is one of the most powerful lines ever penned: "I dwell in possibility."

Where recovery and faith meet, there is possibility.

Jesus said, "Everything is possible for one who believes" (Mark 9:23).

If everything is possible, that means it is possible for you to stay sober for the next twenty-four hours—and the next twenty-four years. It is possible to find lasting freedom and enduring recovery, and to help others find recovery as well.

But there's a catch. This is a promise only for the person "who believes." You can achieve your highest goals in recovery, but only if you are connected to your Higher Power.

Recovery Step: Place your faith in Christ. After that, the possibilities are limitless.

“This Is a Football”

MARCH 8

Every season for his first practice, legendary basketball coach John Wooden took a full hour to teach his players how to properly put on their shoes and socks. In similar fashion, when Vince Lombardi welcomed his new rookies to camp, he held a football in his hand and said, “Gentlemen, this is a football.”

Success begins with the basics—on and off the field.

The Bible says it like this: “Take delight in the Lord, and he will give you the desires of your heart” (Ps. 37:4).

Do you want lasting sobriety from your drug of choice? Start simple and go from there. Love God. Seek him daily. Make him the first priority of every day.

Recovery Step: Return to the basics in your recovery. Get those right, and the rest becomes a whole lot easier.

Procrastination

MARCH 9

Procrastination. It is a curse of the human condition. We all do it; some are just better than others. Mark Twain spoke for all of us when he said, "Never put off till tomorrow what may be done day after tomorrow just as well."

I know firsthand the power of procrastination. That's what got me through college. My mantra was this: Why study for a test tonight when it's not until tomorrow afternoon? That's what God made tomorrow morning for.

That may work in college, but it's a terrible strategy for recovery. If you are to walk in freedom, try the following:

- Do ten minutes of recovery work each morning.
- When you make mistakes, admit them immediately.
- When you are triggered, call someone right then.
- Find a meeting today.

Recovery Step: Paul was unequivocal in his advice. "Whatever you do, work at it with all your heart" (Col. 3:23). Do recovery work heartily. Work hard today so you can walk in freedom tomorrow.

A Million Times Smarter

MARCH 10

Three men died and stood before God. The Lord gave each of them the chance to start a new life on earth with any changes they desired.

The first man said, "Make me a hundred times smarter." So God made him a hundred times smarter for his new life.

The second man said, "I want to be smarter than that guy. Make me a thousand times smarter." God granted his wish.

The third guy said, "I want to be smarter than both of those guys. So make me a million times smarter than I was before."

God granted his wish. The man came back as a woman.

Guys, trust the wisdom, insight, and discernment of your wives. The Old Testament addresses the wisdom of women with these words: "She considers a field and buys it; out of her earnings she plants a vineyard" (Prov. 31:16).

Recovery Step: If you are married, learn to trust your wife.

When Times Are Still Hard

MARCH 11

One of the things many fail to understand early in their recovery is that coming clean and seeking sobriety don't magically make all your problems go away. We say we are all in, and we mean it, but the temptations of our addiction and the suspicions of our friends remain.

There's a great example of this in the Old Testament. The prophet Habakkuk sought God on behalf of his people. He came with a heart of repentance and sincerity. He prayed for God's blessings out of total surrender. And he meant it.

"Though the fig tree does not bud and there are no grapes on the vines, though the olive crop fails and the fields produce no food, though there are no sheep in the pen and no cattle in the stalls, yet I will rejoice in the Lord, I will be joyful in God my Savior. (Hab. 3:17–18).

It's easy to live in sobriety when we are heavily rewarded. But it's what we do when our spouse doesn't come home, when we still lose our job, when our friends still turn away that counts.

Recovery Step: Are times still hard? That's okay. Stay at it. Do the right things. Recovery is its own best reward.

The Power of a Kite

MARCH 12

In 1847, civil engineer Charles Ellet, Jr. was hired to build a bridge over the Niagara Gorge, an 825-foot chasm. He enlisted the help of a sixteen-year-old boy, Homan Walsh, who flew his kite from one side to the other. The day after the successful kite flight, a stronger line was attached to that kite string and pulled across, then a stronger line, then a rope, and then a cable consisting of thirty-six strands of 10-gauge wire. The bridge was eventually built as the world's first railway suspension bridge. It would connect two countries and was strong enough to support a 170-ton locomotive. It all started with a single kite string.

Never underestimate the power of a kite.

The prophet Zechariah said, "Do not despise these small beginnings, for the Lord rejoices to see the work begin, to see the plumb line in Zerubbabel's hand" (Zech. 4:10 NLT).

Don't miss these eight words: "The Lord rejoices to see the work begin."

It's great to be a strong finisher. But guess what matters even more? You need to be a strong starter. You can't finish what you don't start.

Recovery Step: It's time to start the recovery process. Start going to meetings. Start therapy. Start working the Steps. Start on a new book. Start something new.

The Burning Lamp

MARCH 13

We don't always recognize how God does it, but he does it. He provides what we need when we need it, and sometimes not until we need it.

The oil and flour of Zarephath's widow were miraculously available as long as she needed them (1 Kings 17:14–16). After Hezekiah prayed, 185,000 Assyrians were killed by the angel of the Lord without Israel even going to battle (2 Kings 19:35). Gideon defeated the vast army of the Midianites with only 300 men (Judges 7:1–25). Humanly speaking, none of them saw a way out of the situation.

When you come under attack, know this: God will keep your lamp burning.

Recovery Step: Never judge the activity of God by what you see in the moment.

Don't Trip

MARCH 14

Charlie Brown had aspirations to play baseball in the big leagues, but he told Lucy he was afraid he'd never make it. "You've got to start small," Lucy told him. "See if you can walk out onto the mound without falling down."

That's a good place to start. Take the field of play—and life—without falling down.

In recovery, our ultimate goals are well beyond our reach. That's why we must do two things: (1) take it one day at a time, and (2) trust God to do for us what we could not do for ourselves.

That was a hard lesson for Israel to learn. Oppressed, the people feared they would never be strong and independent again. Then God showed up, just in time. God promised to let the armies of Moab, Edom, and Ammon escape his wrath, but not Egypt.

In the Old Testament, Egypt represented captivity for God's people. The prophet Daniel spoke on behalf of God: "He will extend his power over many countries; Egypt will not escape" (Dan. 11:42).

Recovery Step: God promises to do for you what you cannot do for yourself. But you have to get into the game—one day and one pitch at a time.

Burgers

MARCH 15

Every year, Americans eat enough hamburgers that if stacked side by side they would stretch around the earth thirty-two times. That's 50 billion burgers. I did the math. That comes to 156 burgers per person, per year. And that comes to 125,000 calories per person, per year. That equals the suggested calorie intake for two months.

That helps explain why 75 percent of men and 67 percent of women are clinically overweight. While people living in Utah are the thinnest in the United States, the heaviest people are in the state of Louisiana.

Now I'm going to get personal—actually, the Bible is. Paul wrote, "Do you not know that your bodies are temples of the Holy Spirit, who is in you, whom you have received from God?" (1 Cor. 6:19–20).

If your recovery has not affected every part of your life, it is not real recovery. True recovery impacts our lives in a balanced way—sobriety, spiritual life, physical life, emotional well-being, and more.

Recovery Step: Take better care of yourself.

Air Force One

MARCH 16

Until 1956, the Air Force plane carrying the President of the United States was referred to as Air Force 8610. Then something happened that changed everything.

One day, the presidential aircraft was cleared to land at a local airport about the same time as an Eastern Airlines flight, also number 8610. The confusion demanded a change. So from that day forward, the President's plane was designated Air Force One. In fact, it doesn't matter what aircraft he is on. Whatever plane that carries the President is called Air Force One. What makes it special is not the plane but the person on board.

"You, dear children, are from God and have overcome them, because the one who is in you is greater than the one who is in the world" (1 John 4:4).

Through faith in Christ, the Pilot of the universe now sits in your cockpit.

Recovery Step: You can overcome any addiction because of the One in you.

Not Yet

MARCH 17

In my world, people fall into one of two groups. They are either walking in purity and freedom or they want to be. Those who only want to walk in freedom hold onto old habits or are embedded in unhealthy relationships. They want out, but they just aren't ready yet.

Saint Augustine once quipped, "O Lord, help me to be pure, but not yet."

There are a lot of "not yet" addicts. They love the promise of Christ: "Blessed are the pure in heart, for they will see God" (Matt. 5:8). They want to see God. They want to be free. They want to live lives of integrity.

But not yet.

No one can push you into recovery. That is a decision you must make for yourself. If you are in the "not yet" group, ask God to give you a passion for freedom, a passion to see him.

Recovery Step: Are you ready to break free? Are you ready to see God? If your answer is "not yet," ask God to do whatever it takes to move you toward "absolutely!"

Logic vs. Emotions

MARCH 18

Let's talk about logic, emotions, and self-control.

Dr. Jonathan Haidt concluded:

> Your brain consistently tricks you into thinking your logic is in control, but generally, it is not. You are being driven by emotions and instinctual drives which your logical brain then rationalizes. This gives the appearance of the logical mind controlling the subconscious drives. We work hard at gaining self-control, often failing, because of this illusion.

There are two points to be taken from this. First, emotions trump logic. Second, self-control is a commodity we must all pray for, strive for, and never quit pursuing.

The Bible weighs in.

> Old Testament: "Like a city whose walls are broken through is a person who lacks self-control" (Prov. 25:28).

> New Testament: "The fruit of the Spirit is . . . self-control" (Gal. 5:22–23 ESV).

Recovery Step: Never stop pursuing self-control.

The First Traffic Ticket

MARCH 19

The first traffic ticket was issued on May 20, 1899.

You read that right. Taxi driver Jacob German was speeding down Lexington Street in New York City in his Electrobat (fully electric vehicle) at an astounding 12 miles per hour in an 8 mile per hour zone. The bicycle officer who pulled him over arrested him and threw him in jail.

We have been speeding ever since. Each year, 41 million Americans are given tickets for speeding. That's 112,000 per day. Speeding contributes to nearly 10,000 deaths and $41 billion in physical damage per year.

And in case you were wondering, the fastest drivers in America are in Texas where posted speed limits are as high as 85 miles per hour.

Jesus is an advocate for slowing down. He said, "Come to me, all you who are weary and burdened, and I will give you rest" (Matt. 11:28).

Recovery Step: Get out of the fast lane. Slow down and accept God's rest.

Close the Window

MARCH 20

It happened on April 17, 1790. Ben Franklin died from sitting in front of his window. Here's what happened. Franklin was a big believer in fresh air. So every night, he slept with the window open. He wrote, "I rise almost every morning and sit near the window in my chamber without any clothes whatever, half an hour or an hour, according to the season."

April 1790 started like any other time in the eighty-four-year-old's life. But this time, Franklin developed an abscess in his lungs, which his doctors attributed to his many hours sitting naked in front of an open window. The abscess burst on April 17, and he died a few hours later.

Many of us suffer from open windows. We open the window to temptation—just a little—and we are okay, until we're not.

Peter warned, "Keep away from worldly desires that wage war against your very souls" (1 Pet. 2:11 NLT).

It's time to shut the window.

Recovery Step: Identify the open windows of your life. Then do whatever is necessary to nail those windows shut. Your recovery depends on it.

Clouds Without Rain

MARCH 21

I love the imagery found in the short book of Jude. Verse 12 describes false teachers as "shepherds who feed only themselves. They are clouds without rain" (Jude 1:12).

I like that—clouds without rain.

Recovery groups are filled with people like that. They look the part but are just clouds without rain—nice image, poor results. For them, looking good trumps being good.

Psychologist Leon F. Seltzer wrote in his article "Self-Absorption: The Root of All (Psychological) Evil?" in *Psychology Today*, "But though all narcissists and borderlines are self-absorbed, not all self-absorbed individuals warrant being appreciated as portraying either personality disorder. And as I indicated earlier, many *other* personality disturbances can be seen as involving self-absorption (histrionic, paranoid, avoidant, dependent, and obsessive-compulsive)."

Whether he meant to or not, Dr. Seltzer was describing an addict.

Recovery Step: Recovery is about overcoming self-absorption. I leave you with the words of Dr. Martin Luther King, Jr.: "Everybody can be great . . . because everybody can serve."

Gaylord Perry's Moon Shot

MARCH 22

It happened on July 20, 1969. Neil Armstrong became the first human being to step onto the moon.

But something else happened that same day, just a few hours later. Gaylord Perry hit a home run.

What makes that special? In 1963, Alvin Dark, the great pitcher/poor hitter's manager, said, "There'll be a man on the moon before Gaylord Perry hits a home run." Sure enough, that's what happened six years later.

On the day Neil Armstrong stepped onto the moon, Gaylord Perry hit the first home run of his career. He never did it again.

Alvin Dark had a vision that became reality: "Where there is no vision, the people perish" (Prov. 29:18 KJV).

What is your vision for your life? For your marriage? For your sobriety?

> **Recovery Step:** Ask God for a fresh vision of what your life can be if you live it in sobriety.

Just One More Hour

MARCH 23

The next time you are tempted to do something stupid, try this: Wait one hour before you do it.

If ever there was a man who wished he had put off his disobedience for just one more hour, it was King Saul. The Book of 1 Samuel tells the story. Samuel assured the Israelites of God's protection as long as they walked in obedience to him (1 Sam. 12:14).

Then, with Israel off at war, the people became anxious for God to step in. They begged King Saul to offer a sacrifice to God on their behalf. Saul knew that only the priest (Samuel) was allowed to offer this sacrifice. But the war was not going their way, and Samuel was not responding to Saul's messages.

So Saul gave in and offered the sacrifice himself. Within an hour, Samuel arrived, but it was too late. Saul's disobedience would cost him the throne.

If Saul had just waited one more hour, Samuel would have been there, and all would have been great.

What about you? How many times have you had a slip or relapse because you didn't wait one more hour?

Recovery Step: When you are tempted, just wait an hour. God always brings us a way out, in his timing.

Carpe Diem!

MARCH 24

Carpe diem! That Latin phrase means "Seize the day."

Recovery cannot wait another day. If you wait until you are ready, you will never get well. If you wait until the feeling is right, your mood is right, and the timing is right, you will never find sobriety.

The devil doesn't tell you to not enter recovery. That's not his strategy. He tells you, "Get in recovery. Your life depends on it." Then he says, "But wait until tomorrow."

The problem is, tomorrow is the one day you won't find on the calendar.

Carpe diem!

Jesus said, "But about that day or hour no one knows, not even the angels in heaven, nor the Son, but only the Father. As it was in the days of Noah, so it will be at the coming of the Son of Man" (Matt. 24:36–37). He was saying that life is unpredictable. Live for today.

Carpe diem!

Recovery Step: Get started in recovery today. Don't wait another second. *Carpe diem!*

397-Pound Marathoner

MARCH 25

Gerald Schattle tipped the scales at a robust 397 pounds when he made the unexpected decision to run a marathon. His doctors ordered him to lose 100 pounds before his training could begin. Against all odds, he eventually completed a marathon. He didn't set any speed records, but for him, finishing was the goal.

Gerald Schattle finished the race. He met his goal.

Schattle understood what is known as BHAG—big, hairy, audacious goals. His enormous achievement was made possible by one thing: He aimed high. He set a goal and then went for that goal.

That's where greatness begins—with a goal to do something no one else expects you to do. "The plans of the diligent lead surely to abundance, but everyone who is hasty comes only to poverty" (Prov. 21:5 ESV).

Recovery Step: Here's your job. Set a BHAG for your personal sobriety.

The Great Ventriloquist

MARCH 26

Edgar Bergen is widely considered the greatest ventriloquist who ever lived. How did he develop his interest in throwing his voice? As a boy, he ordered a book on photography but received a book on ventriloquism instead. Naturally, he was disappointed. But it was this mix-up that changed everything.

Every successful person I know has taken a major detour in his or her life. For every photographer who became a ventriloquist, there are millions of addicts who became recovering addicts.

How does this change happen? In short, "The Lord directs the steps of the godly" (Ps. 37:23 NLT).

It is our willingness to allow God to redirect our steps that changes everything. If we are willing to take a detour, God will direct our paths.

Recovery Step: Take a hard look at your life. Does something need to change? Does God have a new work to do in your life? Allow this to be the first day of an exciting new journey.

Take One Step

MARCH 27

You must do three things to reach your goals: dream big, start small, and think long. You have to fly the kite a little higher and a little longer each day. Over time, the ceiling becomes the floor.

Emil Zátopek, the great Olympian, said, "Step by step, a man will come to the fifth floor." Zátopek rode that philosophy to three gold medals, winning sixty-nine straight races and running a total of 50,000 miles over his career, the equivalent of two laps around the earth.

I'm not much of a runner unless I'm either chasing something or being chased. But I do walk 10,000 steps every day. The first step is always the hardest.

You will never achieve sobriety a mile at a time. Sobriety is only achieved a step at a time. In fact, God offers an amazing promise for those willing to take life a step at a time: "When you walk, your steps will not be hampered; when you run, you will not stumble" (Prov. 4:12).

> **Recovery Step:** If you want to be in a better place a year from now, take one step in that direction today.

Waterloo

MARCH 28

The Battle of Waterloo was fought on June 18, 1815, near the city of Waterloo in present-day Belgium. All of England knew that the Duke of Wellington was leading the British forces against French Emperor Napoleon Bonaparte in this epic battle. A ship signaled news of the outcome of the battle to a man on top of Winchester Cathedral. The message consisted of three words: "Wellington defeated Napoleon."

But the fog rolled in before the man at the cathedral saw the third word. So the message that went out across England was "Wellington defeated." The British thought they had lost the decisive battle—a battle they had actually won.

Sometimes we get mixed messages. In recovery, we often feel defeated—until we realize this battle is not our own. Our Higher Power has already defeated the enemy. We don't live *for* that victory but *from* it.

Because the battle has already been won, we can say, "To him who is able to keep you from stumbling and to present you before his glorious presence without fault and with great joy" (Jude 1:24).

Recovery Step: Claim the victory that has been secured on the cross.

Life Is a Bicycle

MARCH 29

When I was a kid, I rode my bicycle everywhere. You could do that back then. It was safe to ride through the neighborhood, down any street, and along the bayous. No one asked where I was going; it never occurred to us that riding a bike was unsafe.

There is really just one skill to riding a bike. It's called balance. For those of you who have not yet mastered this athletic specialty, let me give you the secret.

Keep moving.

Albert Einstein said, "Life is like riding a bicycle. To keep your balance, you must keep moving."

Let's repeat that, but let's change one word. "[Recovery] is like riding a bicycle. To keep your balance, you must keep moving."

Recovery Step: Never take a day off from recovery. Heed the words of Job: "The righteous keep moving forward, and those with clean hands become stronger and stronger" (Job 17:9 NLT).

Lou Gehrig

MARCH 30

Lou Gehrig was one of the greatest hitters in the history of baseball, and he was also a true gentleman. He famously never argued with the umpires. That is why one particular game stood out.

After taking a third strike, Gehrig turned to the home plate umpire and said something that no one else could hear. He then walked back to his dugout, noticeably upset.

After the game, reporters asked Gehrig what he had said to the umpire. When he refused to answer, they found the umpire and asked him. The ump laughed as he told them, "He said, 'I wish I had that one over again.'"

That is the story of every sex addict and every relapse. "I wish I had that one over again."

May the hope of a second chance resonate with each of us today: "The Lord's lovingkindnesses indeed never cease, for his compassions never fail. They are new every morning; great is your faithfulness" (Lam. 3:22–23 NASB1995).

> **Recovery Step:** You have a God of a second chance. You may have struck out yesterday, but today, another pitch is on the way. Take advantage of that.

Unoffendable

MARCH 31

Johnny told his friend Jimmy, "You offended me. You should apologize." Jimmy obliged. "Johnny, I am truly sorry . . . that you are so offendable."

Too many of us get too offended by too many people too much of the time. And that's a problem because when we are offended, we become stuck in our recovery.

Living in offended mode is indicative of a lack of forgiveness, and when you don't forgive someone, you are letting those who hurt you define you. That is never a good idea.

Brant Hansen wrote a great book on the subject called *Unoffendable*. He asserts that Christ-followers "should be the most refreshingly unoffendable people on the planet."

Solomon weighs in: "It is to one's glory to overlook an offense" (Prov. 19:11).

Sometimes, being offended can't be helped. But staying offended is a choice. I agree with R. T. Kendall: "The primary way we grieve the Holy Spirit is by fostering bitterness in our hearts."

Recovery Step: The next time someone does something offensive, choose forgiveness over bitterness. Be the most refreshingly unoffendable person you can be.

APRIL

There is nothing noble in being superior to your fellow man.
True nobility lies in being superior to your former self.

—Ernest Hemingway

Just As I Am

APRIL 1

Charlotte Elliott of Brighton, England, was an embittered woman. Her disability had hardened her heart.

"If God loved me," she muttered, "he would not have treated me this way."

Hoping to help her, Swiss minister César Malan visited the Elliotts on May 9, 1822, seeking to calm Charlotte in the midst of her pain. She saw a peace in him that she did not have.

"How do I find that peace?" she asked.

Malan said, "Give yourself to God just as you are."

She did. And years later, describing what had happened, she wrote a poem. "Just as I am, without one plea, but that thy blood was shed for me, and that thou bidst me come to thee, O Lamb of God, I come, I come." That famous hymn became the invitation song Billy Graham used for sixty years of crusades.

Jesus said, "Come to me, all you who are weary and burdened, and I will give you rest" (Matt. 11:28).

Recovery Step: Come to God today—just as you are. Give him your life, your heart, your everything.

The Intruder

APRIL 2

Not long ago, I panicked when I found an intruder in our house. It was early in the morning. I had just finished brushing my teeth when I looked up, and there he was, staring at me. He was the scariest looking man I've seen in a long time. He didn't say anything; he just stared at me as I stared back at him.

My panic turned to relief when I realized who this man was. It was me in the mirror. There I was in all my early morning glory—hair unbrushed, teeth unbrushed, face unwashed. It was hard to look at.

The good news was that there was still time to repair the damage, or at least cover it up. Before facing the world, I did everything in my power to become the person I wanted people to think I looked like rather than who I really was. No one wants to see that.

But at some point, we need to trade in our vanity for reality.

Recovery Step: Yes, we need to clean ourselves up before going out in public. But in recovery, we learn to focus on the more important things. We embrace the words of Solomon who said, "Yet when I surveyed all that my hands had done and what I had toiled to achieve, everything was meaningless, a chasing after the wind; nothing was gained under the sun" (Eccles. 2:11).

The Greatest Boxer

APRIL 3

On September 2, 1892, a boxer named James "Gentleman Jim" Corbett stepped into the ring with John L. Sullivan, arguably the greatest boxer who would ever live. Sullivan was the last heavyweight champion of the bare-knuckle era and the first champion who wore gloves. In fifty fights, he had never lost.

This night would be different. For the only time in his remarkable career, Sullivan lost a fight. Corbett won by knockout in the twenty-first round.

How did Corbett do it? He lived by the mantra, "Fight one more round."

He would later reflect on that fight. "When your arms are so tired that you can hardly lift your hands to come on guard, fight one more round. When your face is bleeding and your eyes are black and you are so tired you wish your opponent would crack you one on the jaw and put you to sleep, fight one more round—remembering that the man who always fights one more round is never whipped."

Recovery Step: Enter the ring of recovery with a plan, not "beating the air" (1 Cor. 9:26). You may never knock out your opponent (lust), but you can win the fight by winning one more round.

Things That Irritate Me

APRIL 4

I think I'm becoming a cranky old guy. At least that's what my neighbor's kid said when I told him to get off my lawn.

These are just a few of the things that drive me crazier than they probably should:

- Walmart shoppers who leave their carts in the middle of the aisle
- Loud music on the beach
- Drivers in the right lane who never turn right
- People who take ten minutes to order at the McDonald's drive-thru
- Men who don't help women with their overhead baggage on an airplane

A friend told me to loosen up. He said, "It's not rocket surgery!" (That's another thing that irritates me—mixed metaphors.)

But my friend had a point. We all need to take stock in what really bothers us. Some things should bother us—rudeness, intolerance, arrogance, and people who drive at night with their headlights off.

But for most things, the Apostle Paul's advice works well: "Keep your head in all situations" (2 Tim. 4:5).

Recovery Step: Chill out.

Heroes

APRIL 5

With all famous people, there is something you didn't know. For example:

- George Washington opened a whiskey distillery.
- Elvis Presley was a natural blond.
- Tim Allen served two years in jail.
- Nicole Kidman is afraid of butterflies.

It gets worse. Think about your personal heroes. I have had several. Many of them are in heaven now. A couple of them are still living, in their nineties. But here's the thing. Heroes have faults. I was rocked to my core when I learned some things about one of my heroes after his death.

There is something about your heroes that you don't know. But don't let that mess you up. The Bible says, "For all have sinned and fall short of the glory of God" (Rom. 3:23). "All" includes heroes.

I never knew that George Washington ran a distillery, but I still see him as a great leader. I didn't know that Tim Allen served time in jail, but that doesn't make him any less funny today.

Let's get real. You have a story most people don't know. So do I. But that doesn't make us less effective tools in the Lord's tool box. In fact, it makes us even more useful in the Potter's hand.

> **Recovery Step:** We've all fallen short. That includes you. But that's okay because Jesus only died for sinners.

The $1 Bike Ride

APRIL 6

"Great job!" my granddad said as he handed me a dollar.

In one ten-minute session, my granddad taught me how to do something my dad had been trying to teach me for over a year—ride a bike without the aid of training wheels. How did he do it? He offered me a dollar.

Here's the lesson. A reward at the end of the journey enhances the chance that the journey will end well.

The same is true of recovery. While the journey itself is reward enough, the thought of hearing my Master say, "Well done, good and faithful servant" (Matt. 25:23) motivates me. But so does the thought of going to bed tonight absent guilt and shame.

Before I made it around the block the first time, I fell a few times. The result was skinned knees and a bruised ego. But I kept at it because the reward of success was worth it.

The same is true in recovery. If you've fallen, get back up. Stay at it, and your progress will lead to victory—a good reward at the end of the journey as well as at the end of today.

Recovery Step: If you've fallen, get back up. Your ride to recovery may include a few falls at first, but you'll eventually make it if you don't give up. And great rewards await.

The Refuge of God

APRIL 7

The words of the old hymn were written in Scotland in 1650.

> God is our refuge and our strength, our ever present aid.
> And, therefore, though the earth remove, we will not be afraid. . . .
> The Lord of hosts is on our side, our safety to secure;
> The God of Jacob is for us, a refuge strong and sure.

Nahum 1:7 says, "The Lord is good, a refuge in times of trouble. He cares for those who trust in him."

Recovery is a very difficult road to walk. Many abandon the journey out of fear, loneliness, or isolation. But when we feel deserted by others, we need to remember that we will never be deserted by God. He is for us, with us, and in us.

You have been humiliated by your addiction. But take heart. Better yet, take refuge in the grace of the God who loves you still.

Recovery Step: In the depths of your addiction, take refuge in God.

Accountability

APRIL 8

Accountability—you can't stay sober without it. But what makes good accountability good?

Peter Bregman, executive coach and best-selling author, wrote an enlightening article, "The Right Way to Hold People Accountable." He suggests five keys to effective accountability:

- Clear expectations
- Clear capability
- Clear measurement
- Clear feedback
- Clear consequences

You need to be accountable to someone. And as you grow in your recovery, you will be the accountability partner to someone else.

Jesus spoke of accountability. He said, "Everyone will have to give account on the day of judgment for every empty word they have spoken" (Matt. 12:36).

The best accountability is what you engage now. Don't wait until the day of judgment to become accountable to someone.

Recovery Step: Review the five keys to effective accountability. Then put them into practice.

C. S. Lewis on Prayer

APRIL 9

As a young man, C. S. Lewis established a strong friendship with a woman named Joy Gresham. It turned to love, and they married. Soon, Joy was diagnosed with cancer. After a hard battle, she died. But there were many ups and downs along the way.

During a period when Joy was responding well to treatment, it was said that a colleague of Lewis's approached him with words of encouragement: "I know how hard you've prayed. God is answering your prayers."

Lewis replied, "I pray because I can't help myself. I pray because I'm helpless. I pray because the need flows out of me all the time, waking and sleeping. It doesn't change God. It changes me."

Most of us pray what I call "outcome prayers." We seek God only for a particular outcome. Well, Joy still died, but C. S. Lewis went on to change the world. But before he changed the world, God changed his heart.

Paul spoke to this need when he said, "In the same way, the Spirit helps us in our weakness. We do not know what we ought to pray for, but the Spirit himself intercedes for us through wordless groans" (Rom. 8:26).

Recovery Step: Are you facing temptations and trials today? Shelve your "outcome prayers" and ask God for the strength equal to the challenge.

Wisdom

APRIL 10

You don't relapse because you don't know what to do. You relapse because you don't do what you know.

Mark Twain was right: "It ain't what you don't know that gets you into trouble."

We don't lack knowledge; we lack wisdom. David prayed, "Bring to an end the violence of the wicked and make the righteous secure—you, the righteous God who probes minds and hearts" (Ps. 7:9).

When facing your next test or temptation, ask yourself three questions:

- What is the wise thing to do?
- What does my friend say is the wise thing to do?
- What do my experiences say is the wise thing to do?

Wisdom trumps knowledge every time. In order to stay sober, you don't need more knowledge; you just need to use the knowledge you already have—wisely.

Recovery Step: Ask God for wisdom.

Unfinished Business

APRIL 11

The shortest book of the New Testament tells us the story of a runaway slave named Onesimus. While in prison, Paul led Onesimus to faith in Christ. But Paul soon discovered that the man had fled from his master, a man named Philemon. While Onesimus was a new man in Christ and while slavery was abhorrent, Paul sent him back to his master to surrender himself to his authority, even though his actions were punishable by death.

Paul wrote a letter to Philemon, which he stuffed in Onesimus's pocket. Imagine the surprise that must have come over Philemon when the fugitive slave returned to his estate. And imagine what went through his mind when he read the letter from Paul, an old friend.

In that letter Paul wrote that Onesimus is "no longer as a slave, but better than a slave, as a dear brother" (Philem. 16).

Philemon gave Onesimus a full pardon.

Your past did not disappear the moment you came to Christ or found sobriety. If you hurt people in your past, you still have unfinished business. It's called making amends. It's called doing the right thing. It's called character. Oh, and another thing, it's also called recovery.

Recovery Step: Think of one person you hurt while you were still a slave to your addiction. Then go to that person and offer your most sincere amends.

Stay Close

APRIL 12

It had been a great day. The disciples of Christ were eye witnesses to the feeding of the 5,000. Now they were riding high and would never look back, right? Wrong. We read, "When evening came, his disciples went down to the lake, where they got into a boat and set off across the lake for Capernaum. By now it was dark, and Jesus had not yet joined them. A strong wind was blowing and the waters grew rough" (John 6:16–18).

We learn two lessons here. First, yesterday's victory is no guarantee of tomorrow's success. They had just witnessed an amazing miracle. Surely, they'd stay on track now. But their newfound faith stayed with them for about two hours.

Second, it is important to wait on God. At the first sign of darkness and pending storms, the disciples left Jesus and went out on their own. They were willing to walk with him as long as they could do it on their own terms.

In recovery, life will be like that of the disciples. In the same day, they witnessed a great miracle and then encountered a harrowing storm. The key to survival is to never walk away from Christ.

Recovery Step: When times are good, walk with Jesus. When times are bad, walk with Jesus. At all times, walk with Jesus.

More to Follow

APRIL 13

Years ago, an anonymous painting of Niagara Falls ended up in a gallery. Because the artist hadn't given the painting a title, the gallery personnel decided to call it *More to Follow*.

That captures the essence of Niagara Falls. Billions of gallons of water have poured over the falls over the years, but we can safely say there is more to follow.

That's the picture of God's grace. There is more to follow. Always there is more to follow.

The Bible says, "But he gives us more grace. That is why Scripture says: 'God opposes the proud but shows favor to the humble'" (James 4:6).

Yesterday you needed God's grace. Today you need God's grace. And tomorrow you will need God's grace. Rest assured, no matter how many times God has already forgiven you, no matter how many times you needed him to bail you out, no matter how much grace your addiction has already required, there is more to follow.

Recovery Step: Claim this promise today: No matter how much God has done for you in the past, there is more to follow.

Harry Callahan

APRIL 14

Harry Callahan spoke the words that have been repeated for decades since. It was 1983. The movie was *Sudden Impact.* Harry Callahan, played by Clint Eastwood, said, "Go ahead, make my day."

The brother of Jesus said it like this: "Anyone who listens to the word but does not do what it says is like someone who looks at his face in a mirror and, after looking at himself, goes away and immediately forgets what he looks like" (James 1:23–24).

In recovery, it is not enough to acknowledge the problem. Recovery requires action. Just as it would be foolish to look in the mirror and not respond, it is foolish to see the road to recovery and not take it. There comes a time when we need to do what Harry said and "go ahead."

Too often we respond to a call to action with inactivity. The task is never complete.

Recovery Step: Knowing what to do is no good unless you follow through with what you know. So take one step forward in your recovery today. Go ahead. Make God's day.

No Gaps Remained

APRIL 15

I've been reading through the Book of Nehemiah. It has long been one of my favorite books of the Bible. But yesterday I came across a little verse that had escaped me until now.

"Sanballat, Tobiah, Geshem the Arab, and the rest of our enemies found out that I had finished rebuilding the wall and that no gaps remained" (Neh. 6:1).

Did you catch the three key words? "No gaps remained."

It took Nehemiah and his men fifty-two days to build the wall around Jerusalem. It was a wall of defense. And it is significant that "no gaps remained" because the wall was only as strong as its weakest point. A huge, fortified wall was useless if just one gap remained, for the enemy would penetrate the city at that gap.

In recovery, it is important to build a wall of defense. We do that by going to meetings, reading recovery material, practicing spiritual disciplines, and more. But none of this will keep us sober if just one gap remains.

Recovery Step: Is there a gap in your recovery? If so, stop everything else you are doing until you fortify that gap.

Mired in the Weeds

APRIL 16

The date was October 13, 1960. Andy Jerke was just like every other boy growing up in Pittsburgh. He loved baseball and especially the Pirates. On that day, the Pirates were hosting the vaunted New York Yankees for game seven of the World Series. The game came down to the bottom of the ninth inning. The score was tied. And Andy was there at Forbes Field.

Then he remembered he had promised his mother to be home by 4:30 p.m. to help with dinner. So he left the game in the bottom of the ninth to walk home.

As he was walking across the lot beyond the outfield wall, a baseball landed near his feet. Andy picked up the ball, and a security guard informed him that Bill Mazeroski had just hit that ball for a game-winning home run. And now the ball belonged to Andy.

Andy played with the ball a year later and lost it in a field. He looked for it for ten minutes and then gave up. What happened to the ball? It got mired in the weeds.

Jesus said, “As the weeds are pulled up and burned in the fire, so it will be at the end of the age” (Matt. 13:40).

Recovery Step: Watch out for the little things that can trip you up. Don’t get mired in the weeds.

Life Jackets

APRIL 17

As a storm raged, the captain realized his ship was sinking fast. He called out, "Anyone here know how to pray?"

One man stepped forward. "Aye, Captain, I know how to pray."

"Good," said the captain. "You pray while the rest of us put on our life jackets. We're one short."

In life—and recovery—it's a good thing to know how to pray. In fact, I tell all my clients to pray three prayers three times a day: Serenity Prayer, 3rd Step Prayer, and 7th Step Prayer. But there comes a time when we need to go to work on our recovery. If we don't, like the guy on that ship, we will eventually drown.

Success comes to those who pray as though it all depends upon God. But then they work as though it all depends upon themselves. The words of James ring true: " If anyone, then, knows the good they ought to do and doesn't do it, it is sin for them" (James 4:17).

Recovery Step: You need to know what to do. But mostly, you just need to do what you know.

Blindness

APRIL 18

One of the first steps toward recovery is the recognition of your problem. It is only when we see our addiction that we can address it. Sight is everything.

There once lived a prophet named Zephaniah. He wrote perhaps the most obscure book in the Bible, bearing his name. The theme of the book is "the day of the Lord." It is a book about judgment. Zephaniah came along a generation after the Southern Kingdom had turned its back on its covenant obligations toward Yahweh, resulting in exile. Zephaniah's message to the people was to turn to God or there would be no hope for their future.

In his message, Zephaniah pronounced God's harshest judgment. "I will bring such distress on all people that they will grope about like those who are blind, because they have sinned against the Lord" (Zeph. 1:17).

Did you catch that? God's judgment was not the destruction of their crops or economy; it was not a curse on their people or their livelihood. What was God's greatest threat?

Blindness. There is nothing worse than the inability to see things as they are.

Recovery Step: Ask God to remove your blinders, to let you see yourself as you really are. Then respond by seeking the face of the One who can renew, repair, and restore.

She Died at 122

APRIL 19

Jeanne Calment's record is still intact, though Kane Tanaka gave it a good ride.

A few years ago, Tanaka died at the age of 119. But she fell short of Jeanne Calment's record of 122 years, making her the only person verified to have eclipsed the age of 120. Calment lived from 1875 to 1997.

The key to her longevity? She said, "I quit smoking when I turned 117."

Jeanne also maintained a routine of morning prayer, beginning at 6:45 a.m. each day.

That's not a bad recipe for life—quit your addiction and keep on praying.

The Bible says it like this: "Pray without ceasing" (1 Thess. 5:17 ESV).

Recovery Step: I can't promise you that if you (a) quit your addiction and (b) pray each morning you will live to be 122. But I can promise you that however long you do live, it will be better.

The Naked Truth

APRIL 20

Garry Shandling said, "My friends tell me that I have an intimacy problem. But they don't really know me."

I can relate. I'll never forget the first time I heard that sexual addiction is an intimacy disorder. I was having breakfast with a man who has a recovery ministry. He mentioned, "Of course, sexual addiction is an intimacy disorder." On the outside, I nodded in agreement. On the inside, I thought, "This dude is wacked!"

No one wants to admit to an addiction. And even fewer want to admit to an "intimacy disorder." But it's true. And the quicker we face that fact, the sooner we can address it.

The Bible attacks this head on.

"And no creature is hidden from his sight, but all are naked and exposed to the eyes of him to whom we must give account" (Heb. 4:13 ESV).

Recovery Step: We are all naked before God. When becoming naked before others, be careful and very selective. There are other parts of your person you do need to expose to others—your heart, soul, and spirit, for example.

No More Secrets

APRIL 21

George Orwell said, "If you want to keep a secret, you must also hide it from yourself."

Secrets kill.

Isaiah 29:15 reads, "Woe to those who go to great depths to hide their plans from the Lord, who do their work in darkness and think, 'Who sees us? Who will know?'"

Secrets kill.

André Malraux said, "Man is not what he thinks he is, he is what he hides."

Secrets kill.

Dr. Michael Slepian, professor at Columbia Business School, has written extensively on the power of secrets. He warns that we can become too good at keeping secrets, making that—keeping the secrets—the goal. In thinking so much about the secrets we are seeking to protect, we keep thinking about the very secrets that lead to relapse.

Even your darkest, most intimate secrets must come to light. Why? Because secrets kill.

Recovery Step: It is critical to get your secrets out. In 12-Step work, this is called "working the First Step." You must let go of your secrets—because secrets kill.

Relapse Rate

APRIL 22

I hate it when someone drops out of one of my Freedom Groups. My first reaction is, "What did I do wrong?" Over the years I have been leading groups, we have grown from five groups to twelve, and from fifty men to 200. But I always fret over the one who slips away.

Then I read this verse and realize I'm in good company. "From this time many of his disciples turned back and no longer followed him" (John 6:66).

There will always be a significant number of addicts who drop out before they cross the finish line. The statistics are alarming.

In a one-year period, a certain treatment center reported that 70.2 percent of their patients dropped out before completing the program.

Another study found that when people leave an inpatient treatment center, 40–60 percent relapse within thirty days.

Further research concludes that the relapse rate for the first year of recovery is 85 percent.

A survey of Alcoholics Anonymous members found that once sober for five years, the relapse rate drops to just 7 percent.

Recovery Step: Relapse is a lot easier than recovery. But relapse is always a bad choice. Stay in your program. Keep moving forward. You've come too far to drop out now.

Fast and Furious

APRIL 23

There's a great line from the movie *The Fast and the Furious*: "I live my life a quarter mile at a time."

Dr. Eric Maisel wrote, "Recovery requires daily exercises and paying daily attention to your life's purposes."

If you desire long-term sobriety, I offer this advice: Stop it!

Let me explain. While long-term sobriety must be the objective, it must never be the goal. Aim for twenty-four hours. When tomorrow comes—if it does—aim for twenty-four hours all over again. The battle is won one day at a time, one temptation at a time, and one decision at a time.

Make each new day your now day. Live in the moment. Celebrate the promise of God: "His mercies never come to an end; they are new every morning" (Lam. 3:22).

Recovery Step: Live your life a quarter mile at a time.

Dog Bites

APRIL 24

A dog bit a man, and it was determined that the dog had rabies. When the man's doctor told him the news, the man sat down and began to write a list of names.

"What are you writing?" asked the doctor.

The man responded, "I'm making a list of all the people I want to bite."

When we have been bitten, our natural response is often to bite someone else. No one wants to suffer alone. And we certainly want our enemies to suffer at least as much as we have.

This is especially true for addicts. No one chooses addiction. For most of us, we were heavily affected by the inappropriate actions of family, friends, or even strangers. It is natural to want to bite back.

But another person's pain never makes our pain any less. The Bible says, "Do not take revenge, my dear friends, but leave room for God's wrath, for it is written: 'It is mine to avenge; I will repay,' says the Lord" (Rom. 12:19).

Recovery Step: When you are in pain, do your best to process that pain in a healthy way.

Practice

APRIL 25

After retiring from coaching, John Wooden was asked what he missed most. I'll give you a hint: it wasn't the games, trophies, or championships. In a word, Wooden said what he missed most was practice.

As a chaplain for the Houston Rockets, I often sat on the sideline watching the players go through their pregame practice. I was stunned to see the discipline and routine that James Harden committed himself to ninety minutes before every game when no one was in the arena to watch. As a result, he led the NBA in scoring and was named the league's Most Valuable Player.

Practice. It's huge—in any sport.

Paul wrote to the church, "Whatever you have learned or received or heard from me, or seen in me—put it into practice" (Phil. 4:9).

Success is the result of practice. That is especially true in the arena we call recovery.

Recovery Step: Practice recovery routines with great diligence this week.

Some

APRIL 26

I recently came across a little verse in one of the least quoted books of the Bible: 2 John. As one of the early followers of Christ, John was checking up on the development of new believers. Word came back to him. Notice his response.

"It has given me great joy to find some of your children walking in the truth, just as the Father commanded us" (2 John 1:4).

One word really jumps out at me—*some*. John found great joy in learning that some of Christ's followers were still walking in the truth.

Here's my take on that. Not everyone who begins the road of discipleship will stay on that road to the end. Some will, but not all. The same is true of recovery. Some, not all, will continue to walk the road of sobriety. And for John, that is worthy of celebration.

If you know the power of addiction, you get this. What's amazing isn't that some fall back into relapse but that some do not.

Recovery Step: Praise God for those in your life who have not fallen back into their addiction.

Let's Roll!

APRIL 27

"Are you guys ready? Okay. Let's roll." Those were Todd Beamer's last recorded words.

The passengers who counterattacked the hijackers of United Flight 93 on September 11, 2001, demonstrated that when a crisis strikes, ordinary people often rise to the occasion. The heroic actions of this group who took a stand against the hijackers probably prevented the destruction of another historic Washington, DC, building—either the U.S. Capitol or the White House.

In a taped phone conversation, Todd Beamer recited the Lord's Prayer and Psalm 23. Then he prayed, "Jesus, help me" before leading the attack on the hijackers. Undoubtedly, Beamer and his fellow passengers were scared. But faced with this challenge, his faith in Christ kicked in. He took action, uttering those now famous words, "Let's roll." Although Beamer's story ended tragically in a farmer's field in Shanksville, Pennsylvania, it stands as an inspiration to all who will never forget the shock of that infamous day.

Like Beamer's courageous call to action, Queen Esther's statement "If I perish, I perish" (Esther 4:16) perfectly expresses the do-or-die quality of active faith. Esther's decision to speak on behalf of her threatened people, knowing that the king could execute her, demonstrates that God provides courage in crises to people who are willing to step out in faith.

Recovery Step: It's time to take a stand in the face of the enemy. All of heaven is on your side. "Let's roll!"

Dead Ringer

APRIL 28

A man with no arms was in need of a job. He walked into a large Catholic parish and inquired of the priest, "Do you have any jobs for me?"

The priest answered, "Only one. We need someone to ring the bell in the tower. If you are able to climb to the top and ring the bell each hour, the job is yours."

The armless man gladly accepted. He climbed to the top of the tower. Each hour, he rang the huge bell—with his face. He had no other way so he ran into the bell at the top of each hour with his face. Sadly, one day he missed the bell and fell out of the tower to his death.

When police arrived, they questioned several onlookers. They asked if anyone recognized the dead man with no arms. One witness responded, "I don't know him personally, but his face rings a bell."

Now, I'll take that awful joke and bend it into a lesson. Let's try this: The armless man is an example of how much you can accomplish in life if you only use your head.

Recovery Step: Use your head—as in ask for wisdom. Do what Solomon did when God offered him anything he wanted. Solomon asked for wisdom (1 Kings 3:12).

The Idol of Sobriety

APRIL 29

I'm going to say something shocking. Ready? Here goes.

Sobriety can become an idol.

Yes, you read that correctly. Sobriety can become an idol. John Piper defined an idol as "anything that we come to rely on for some blessing, or help, or guidance in the place of a wholehearted reliance on the true and living God."

By that standard, sobriety can become an idol. Sobriety is a good thing, but it's not the main thing. Here are just three things that are more important than your sobriety:

- Your recovery
- Daily habits
- God

The Ten Commandments include this little gem: "Do not turn to idols" (Lev. 19:4). In other words, make sobriety a means to your goal (godliness) but not the ultimate goal itself. Even good things can become idols. Never let anything stand between you and your God.

Recovery Step: Let sobriety be a goal, but not the goal.

Read It and Run

APRIL 30

"Write the vision; make it plain on tablets, so he may run who reads it" (Hab. 2:2 ESV).

That gem from Habakkuk, a minor prophet, has echoed throughout the chambers of time. Its message is timeless. He is simply saying that once you get a clear vision of your destiny, you can sprint in the right direction with confidence.

Seneca said, "There is no favorable wind for the sailor who doesn't know where to go."

You will never go farther in life—or recovery—than you can see. That requires vision. Let me offer three keys to a great vision:

- Destination: Where am I going?
- Purpose: Why am I doing this?
- Values: What principles do I live by?

Recovery Step: If you don't have a clear vision for your future, commit your life to finding that vision. Then go for it and never look back.

MAY

Life is a matter of choices, and every choice you make makes you.

—John Maxwell

Old Man Rocking

MAY 1

A woman walked up to a little old man rocking in a chair on his porch. "I couldn't help noticing how happy you look," she said. "What's your secret to a long, happy life?"

The man replied, "I smoke three packs of cigarettes a day. I also drink a case of whiskey, eat fatty foods, and never exercise."

The woman responded in amazement, "So just how old are you?"

The man answered, "Twenty-six."

We are not always what we appear.

The Bible says, "Man looks on the outward appearance, but the Lord looks on the heart" (1 Sam. 16:7 ESV).

Recovery Step: Never assume anyone else is doing as well—or as poorly—as they appear. Get involved. Ask questions. Be their friend.

Hypocrisy

MAY 2

Hamlet said to Ophelia, "God has given you one face, and you make yourself another."

Addicts are hypocrites. They have to keep things in order to maintain the ruse. Addicts live the normal life in front of the audience they know while living a different life backstage.

Those in church leadership are not immune. Paul wrote of such in his letter to Titus. "They claim to know God, but by their actions they deny him. They are detestable, disobedient and unfit for doing anything good" (Titus 1:16).

That's strong language!

Indian monk Swami Vivekananda wrote in his *Meditation and Its Methods,* "It is better to be an outspoken atheist than a hypocrite."

If you are in church leadership or simply a Christ-follower, know this. You are being watched. The question the world is asking is this: Is the person they see really the person you are? It is only when we get real that we get right. Today is a pretty good time to start.

Recovery Step: It's time to start living the life you say you live. You have a God of second chances. So come clean with someone this week. And know this: There is nothing you have ever done that has made God love you less.

Plan, Plan, Plan

MAY 3

Dr. David Susman, clinical psychologist, has written a helpful article called "10 Keys to Recovery." One of his keys to recovery is this:

Develop a plan.

Susman explains, "Without direction, it's impossible to get from point A to point B. Your plan should include your overall goals and specific action steps for getting there. Your plan must be written down to make it 'real' and so you won't forget all the details. Give copies of your plan to your key supporters so they can help hold you accountable and keep encouraging you as you move forward."

God is the great Planner. He told the prophet Jeremiah, "For I know the plans I have for you" (Jer. 29:11).

You need a recovery plan. It should probably include weekly recovery meetings, daily devotions, daily exercise, Step work, spiritual disciplines, church attendance, accountability, protection of your devices, financial guardrails, therapy, and more.

Your plan needs to be practical, specific, and measurable. There is no better time to develop your personal recovery plan than right now.

> **Recovery Step:** Develop a recovery plan today.

Routine

MAY 4

One of the keys to making good habits is to establish good routines. But once the routine becomes routine, you have to change it. That is known as the law of requisite variety. For example, if you always work out the same way, your workout will eventually lose its effectiveness as your body adapts to the routine. You have to confuse your muscles by interrupting the pattern.

We serve a God who said, "I am doing a new thing" (Isa. 43:19). Here are a few things you might want to switch up:

- Attend a new meeting.
- Find a new recovery partner.
- Read a new book.
- Rework an old Step.
- Look for a new podcast.
- Do a Recovery Day.

Recovery Step: Think of something today that you can change tomorrow.

Samaria

MAY 5

"[Jesus] had to go through Samaria" (John 4:4).

Let me explain why this matters.

The Jews and Samaritans disliked each other. It all went back to 722 BC when the Assyrians conquered Israel and took the Northern ten tribes into captivity. They brought in Gentiles from other areas to settle in that same region. Eventually, those Gentiles with their pagan ways intermarried with the Jews who had been left behind. Over the generations, they developed their own religion and eventually built their own temple.

When Jesus prepared to travel from Judea (in the south) to Galilee (in the north), he had a dilemma. The most direct route would take him through Samaria, but this was the last place a Jew would normally go. Samaritans hated Jews, and Jews hated Samaritans.

So why did Jesus have to go through Samaria? It was simple. He knew that on this route he would encounter a woman at Jacob's well who was in desperate need to know the Savior.

Recovery Step: Do you find yourself in Samaria today? Don't fight it. Accept your form of Samaria as part of God's overarching plan for your life.

Billy Martin

MAY 6

On October 19, 1987, Billy Martin was named manager of the New York Yankees . . . for the fifth time.

In order for Billy Martin to be named Yankees manager five times, he had to set another record first. He was fired as manager of the Yankees four times.

It was Martin's response to disappointment and not the disappointments themselves that defined him. As a player, Billy Martin was traded seven times. As a manager of seven different teams, he was fired ten times. But Martin was also an All-Star (1956) and won five World Series as a player and manager. His number was retired by the Yankees. They even erected a statue in his honor at Yankee Stadium.

Never underestimate the power of resilience, especially in recovery.

The Bible says it like this: "Be strong and courageous. Do not be afraid; do not be discouraged" (Josh. 1:9).

Recovery Step: Have you hit bottom? Then it's time to bounce back.

Dial Louder

MAY 7

Charles Schultz debuted his first-ever "Peanuts" comic strip on October 2, 1950, in nine newspapers across America. Over the next six decades, Schultz produced 18,000 more comic strips. The wisdom of Charlie Brown, Lucy, Linus, and the whole gang has guided many of us through the challenges of life.

One of those challenges—especially for those of us in recovery—is to stay at the hard work necessary to find success. We give up too early.

Lucy has the answer. "If no one answers the phone, dial louder."

Paul said it like this. "To those who by persistence in doing good seek glory, honor and immortality, he will give eternal life" (Rom. 2:7).

The fact is that the road to recovery will encounter many storms. The answer is not to pull over but to keep driving. It's about persistence. It's about determination. Stay at it. Keep driving. Dial louder.

Recovery Step: As you encounter trials and temptations, keep moving forward. That is the only way out of the storm.

Addiction Test

MAY 8

Most of our readers are either some kind of addict or are married to one. But some of you, while struggling with compulsive behaviors, are not yet certain if you really qualify as an addict. Since there is no blood test for addiction, a diagnosis will always include a level of subjectivity.

But for most of us, it becomes pretty clear. If you aren't one of those, if you aren't certain that you are an addict, we can help. The following five criteria are consistent among addicts. If at least four of them describe you, you can be sure you have a problem.

- You consistently cross your own moral code with your personal behaviors.
- Your fantasies of acting out make it difficult to concentrate on daily tasks.
- You keep your activities a secret.
- You feel enormous shame after acting out but continue to do so anyway.
- You have tried to stop many times without lasting success.

How many of these describe you? If you are an addict, seek help. Reach out to us today. We can help.

Recovery Step: "How gracious he will be when you cry for help!" (Isa. 30:19).

30 Days

MAY 9

Can you stay sober for the next thirty days?

I remember when such a goal seemed crazy. It was on par with becoming an Olympic swimmer or NASA scientist, or watching a Hallmark movie without jumping off a tall building.

Impossible.

I love what Nelson Mandela said. "It always seems impossible until it is done."

The king of quotes went even further: "With God all things are possible" (Matt. 19:26).

So I ask you again: Can you stay sober for the next thirty days? Of course you can! There are millions of recovering addicts who have been sober for five, ten, or fifteen years. And every one of them has one thing in common.

They all stayed sober for the first thirty days.

Recovery Step: Thirty days of sobriety is not a matter of chance; it is a matter of choice. And you can make that choice, starting right now.

Progress

MAY 10

"I am the Lord your God, who brought you out of Egypt so that you would no longer be slaves to the Egyptians; I broke the bars of your yoke and enabled you to walk with heads held high" (Lev. 26:13).

As with the Israelites' sojourn to Egypt, the wilderness, and eventually the Promised Land, recovery is a long, winding journey.

The transtheoretical model of change (TTM) offers five stages of recovery: precontemplation, contemplation, preparation, action, and maintenance.

Let me simplify that. We think about thinking about it, we think about it, we prepare for it, we take steps toward recovery, and we maintain the ground we have gained.

Where are you in the recovery process? Chances are that you are somewhere between thinking about thinking about it and maintaining total success. You aren't where you're gonna be, but you aren't where you used to be either. Thank God for the progress. Then take the next right step—one day at a time.

Recovery Step: You aren't where you're gonna be, and you aren't where you used to be. Celebrate the progress you have already made and keep moving forward. Your Promised Land awaits.

A Rope

MAY 11

A hiker was walking down a country road one day when he heard a voice in the distance. "Help me! Someone help me now!"

As the hiker followed the direction of the voice, he eventually came upon a horrifying scene. A man had fallen into a sea of quicksand and was flailing helplessly as he slowly sank toward a terrible death.

The hiker had to make a quick decision. He had two options:

- Throw the man a rope and pull him to safety.
- Lecture the man on what he had done wrong.

Often we spend too much time telling others what they did wrong and not enough time throwing them a rope. That is especially true with addicts. While it may be true that they have made a lot of bad decisions, it is also true that they need a rope.

Nehemiah understood this principle when he prayed, "Whenever your people turned and cried to you again for help, you listened once more from heaven. In your wonderful mercy, you rescued them many times!" (Neh. 9:28 NLT).

Recovery Step: When you see someone in trouble, offer them a rope rather than a speech.

The Last Thing Charley Did

MAY 12

A terrible explosion rocked a gunpowder factory. After the mess was cleaned up, the inquiry began. One of the survivors was pulled into the investigator's office and asked, "Okay, Simpson. You were near the scene, so tell me what happened."

"Well, it was like this, sir. Old Charley Higgins was in the mixing room, and I saw him pull a cigarette from his pocket and light it up."

The investigator responded, "Are you telling me Higgins was smoking in the mixing room? How long had he been with the company?"

"About twenty years, sir."

"Well, he should have known better! You'd think lighting a cigarette in the mixing room would have been the last thing he would do."

"It was, sir."

Here's the lesson. In recovery, our problem is not a lack of knowledge. We are seldom at a loss for what we should avoid in life. Paul wrote, "The acts of the flesh are obvious: sexual immorality, impurity, and debauchery" (Gal. 5:19).

Recovery Step: You know the things to do and the things to avoid. Recovery is the alignment of right knowledge and right actions. The next move is yours.

Step 1

MAY 13

Dr. David Deyhimy, Medical Director of the Edge Treatment Center, cites recent data on addiction. His findings include the following:

- 45 million Americans are directly affected by addiction.
- 23 million Americans are in some form of addiction recovery.
- One-third of all households have one addict living there.

Addiction is a pandemic on many levels. Your first job if you are an addict is to admit the magnitude of the problem. You must get honest and tell someone, "I have a problem, and I can't fix this on my own."

Jesus said, "The truth will set you free" (John 8:32).

The fact that you have a behavioral or substance addiction is a hard truth to swallow. But until you do, recovery will only be a mirage.

Recovery Step: There is only one Step that you need to work perfectly. It's Step 1. Say it with me now. "I admit that I am powerless over my addiction and my life has become unmanageable."

Talk to Your Mountain

MAY 14

If you haven't read the Book of Zechariah in a while, you missed this gem from God's Word.

"What are you, mighty mountain?" (Zech. 4:7).

When was the last time you talked to your mountain? Mountains represent huge challenges that God intends for us to overcome. That's why I have this hanging on my wall: "Your mountain awaits, so get on your way!"

Chris Nikic knows a little about talking to mountains. On November 7, 2020, he became the first person with Down syndrome to finish the Ironman Triathlon. In sixteen hours and forty-seven minutes, Chris swam 2.4 miles, cycled 112 miles, and ran 26.2 miles. How did Chris Nikic train for such an extraordinary achievement? It was easy. He said, "I tried to improve by 1 percent each day."

Recovery is a mountain worth climbing. How can you make it? Improve by 1 percent each day.

Recovery Step: Talk to your mountain. Then improve by 1 percent each day.

The Farmhouse

MAY 15

There was a preacher who saved up enough money to buy some cheap land. On it stood a dilapidated farmhouse. For a year, the preacher refurbished the house on his days off. Once the work was complete, a neighbor came over and said, "Well, preacher, I have to hand it to you. It looks like you and the Lord have done a pretty good job with this place."

Wiping the sweat from his brow, the preacher said, "Yeah, I suppose we have. But you should have seen the place when the Lord had it all to himself."

The Bible says, "We are God's fellow workers" (1 Cor. 3:9 ESV).

There is an old statement we say in recovery work. "Without God, I can't. Without me, God won't."

Recovery is like any other great undertaking. To be successful, there must be a partnership. God could make us right without our participation, but he won't. And we could get right on our own except for one thing: We really can't.

Recovery Step: Are you ready to get well? The only limit to the success of your recovery will be your resistance to partner with God to make it happen.

Bagpipes

MAY 16

A college freshman was struggling to keep up with his classwork assignments. When his parents came to visit, they asked him what the problem was.

He said, "The guys in the apartment above me keep their TV up too loud. I can't concentrate."

His parents asked, "What do you do when they get too loud?"

College student: "I just go back to playing my bagpipes."

That's how a lot of us think. We don't notice our own problems because we focus on the weaknesses of others. Jesus has a better plan: "First take the plank out of your own eye, and then you will see clearly to remove the speck from your brother's eye" (Matt. 7:5).

Try this. For the next seven days, don't even think about anyone else's shortcomings. Ask the Holy Spirit to shine his light on your issues, the things you need to address.

Recovery Step: You must take ownership of your disease if you are to take responsibility for your recovery.

Shakespeare's Illiterate Parents

MAY 17

William Shakespeare remains one of the most famous playwrights and poets of all time. And while he attended grammar school to master reading, writing, and Latin, his parents and children were almost entirely illiterate. The ability to read and write wasn't necessary during the Elizabethan era, and while Shakespeare's father, John, might have had a basic level of literacy, he signed his name with a mark instead of his full name. William's two daughters could not read or write at all.

Things are not necessarily passed down from generation to generation.

You are not doomed to a life of addiction because your mom or dad was an addict. The same goes for your children. The Bible speaks of "generational sins" (Exod. 20, 34; Deut. 5). It's important to understand the context.

In Old Testament times, no one ever left home, so kids were raised in the home of their parents and grandparents. Rather than being exposed to parental behaviors for eighteen years, it was for life. So the lifestyles of their immediate family members carried profound significance.

Recovery Step: Do not live in the shadow of another person's addiction. Chart a new path.

Joe DiMaggio

MAY 18

When World War II ended, Joe DiMaggio returned home. Not yet ready to resume his baseball career, he took his son, Joe, Jr., to a Yankees game. The Yankee legend wore sunglasses and a ball cap, hoping to go unnoticed.

Eventually, the Yankee Clipper was recognized by the fans. They stood and chanted, "Joe, Joe DiMaggio! Joe, Joe DiMaggio!"

Hearing the thunderous crowd, Joe, Jr. looked up at his dad and said, "See, Daddy, everyone here knows my name!"

Of course, the adulation was intended for Joe, Sr. That's where we get into trouble—when we take the glory intended for our Father. We can never take credit for the recovery that only God makes possible. We often refer to the "gift of sobriety" because that's what it is—a gift. And behind every gift is a giver.

Like Joe DiMaggio, Jr., we are made in the image of our Father. "God created mankind in his own image" (Gen. 1:27). We must be content to be in his image, in his shadow. It is when we define ourselves by what we have done instead of by whose we are that we get into trouble.

Recovery Step: Recovery starts where pride leaves off. When we realize who we are and who God is, we have just taken the first step in our recovery.

Arnold Palmer's Golf Club

MAY 19

In 1970, Arnold Palmer played golf with the king of Saudi Arabia. After their time together, the king wished to express his appreciation to the golfing legend. He asked Palmer if there was anything he could give him as a token of his appreciation.

Palmer said, "I guess if you really want to, you can give me a golf club."

A couple of weeks passed, and Arnold Palmer received a small package from Saudi Arabia. When he opened it, he read the card, which said, "A gift from the king." Then he discovered his gift inside that card—a certificate proving his ownership of a golf club in Saudi Arabia, all eighteen holes.

God "is able to do immeasurably more than all we ask or imagine" (Eph. 3:20).

Recovery Step: When you pray, remember the size of your king. While you are praying for a golf club, God is waiting to give you a golf club!

The First Roller-Coaster

MAY 20

People have been looking for ways to blow money since the Lydian lion coin was created 2,700 years ago. In slightly more modern times, tourists couldn't resist the urge to ride the world's first roller-coaster, even if it cost them something.

Actually, it wasn't supposed to be a roller-coaster. When tourists witnessed rail cars transporting coal at speeds up to 50 miles per hour, they offered a few cents for the opportunity to ride along for the fun.

The need for speed has never left us. But those thrills come with a price tag attached.

Solomon warned, "Whoever loves pleasure will become poor" (Prov. 21:17).

So here's my question. Does God have control of your finances? I suggest that God will never be Lord at all until he is Lord of all. Your recovery will never be strong if you put pleasure ahead of financial obedience.

Recovery Step: Surrender your money to the Lord.

Green Apples

MAY 21

I read somewhere, "How could I possibly be the apple of God's eye when my behavior is not yet perfect? Because green apples are apples, too. One day I shall be a mature September apple, perfectly formed. But for now, I am still growing."

God's love transcends our shortcomings. He promises, "I have loved you with an everlasting love; therefore I have continued my faithfulness to you" (Jer. 31:3 ESV).

One of the keys to recovery is patience. God is at work in us, whether we see it or not. And he works on his terms and in his timing.

Phillips Brooks, the famous New England pastor of the late 1800s, was once spotted pacing the floor like a caged animal. A friend asked him what was wrong. Brooks responded, "The trouble is I'm in a hurry, but God isn't!"

Recovery Step: You are the apple of God's eye, whether you are ripe yet or not. Trust in God's unfinished work in your life, not because you are good but because he is.

Drawing Jesus

MAY 22

A little boy was drawing a picture. When his father asked him what he was sketching, he replied, "I'm drawing a picture of God." The father said with a smile, "Son, no one knows what God looks like." The little boy declared, "They will when I'm done!"

Somehow, children are able to draw a picture of God that adults could never draw. Jesus went even further when "he called a little child to him, and placed the child among them. And he said: 'Truly I tell you, unless you change and become like little children, you will never enter the kingdom of heaven'" (Matt. 18:2–3).

Catch these three important words: "unless you change."

God does not enter a life that he does not change. Let me say it another way. We have a come-as-you-are Savior, but he is not a stay-as-you-are Lord.

Recovery Step: If you are serious about life transformation, submit to God with a childlike faith that changes us from the inside out.

Dollhouse

MAY 23

A little girl climbed onto her daddy's lap and asked him to build her a dollhouse. Much to her delight, he promised to do so. Then he left town for an extended business trip. When he returned, he entered his daughter's room to find all her dolls and doll furniture packed in boxes. When he asked her about it, she said she had packed for the upcoming move into the new dollhouse.

Although her father had not yet built the dollhouse and though the daughter could see no physical evidence that he ever would, she took him at his word and prepared for the upcoming move, not knowing exactly when that would take place.

Jesus promised that after he went away, he would prepare our "dollhouse." "And if I go and prepare a place for you, I will come back and take you to be with me that you also may be where I am" (John 14:3).

I know two things about this "dollhouse."

It will be free of all temptation.

God is working on it, whether you can see it or not.

Recovery Step: Walk in freedom, knowing that things are about to get a whole lot better.

American Idol

MAY 24

One of the most popular TV shows of the last two decades is *American Idol.* It is in our nature to seek idols. I grew up idolizing Willie Mays. In my teen years, everyone I knew had posters on their walls representing their personal idols such as Patrick Swayze from *Dirty Dancing* or the best-selling poster of all time, the 1976 *Life* magazine cover featuring Farrah Fawcett.

John Calvin said, "Every one of us, even from his mother's womb, is a master craftsman of idols."

It's in our nature.

The Bible warns us, "Dear children, keep yourselves from idols" (1 John 5:21). It's one of the Ten Commandments. Repeatedly, the Bible warns us to avoid idols.

An idol is something we can see, but it never fulfills. The list of examples is endless: money, fame, success, another person. Or how about this one: addiction. Every addict has made an idol out of his obsession. The problem is that it never fulfills.

Recovery Step: Identify your idol. Know this: What you idolize today, you worship tomorrow. And then it owns you.

Limp

MAY 25

In the Old Testament, we read the story about Jacob wrestling with God (Gen. 32:22–32). At one point, God wounded Jacob's hip, leaving him with a lingering limp. Jacob was suddenly in a position of helplessness. He would live with that limp for the rest of his life.

I can relate. My addiction is my limp. And while I've learned to walk with it, that weakness, that limp, is never far from my mind.

The limp can be a great teacher.

My limp has become my blessing in three ways:

- It reminds me I must rely on God.
- It reminds me of the damage I can cause.
- It helps me relate to other men who walk with a limp.

Even in the midst of your no-win situation, God is there. In fact, he often uses a crisis to get your attention. God whispers to you in your pleasure, but he shouts to you in your pain.

Recovery Step: Let God use your limp to draw you closer to him.

Recovery Rewards

MAY 26

What role do rewards play in recovery?

Dr. John F. Kelly addresses this in his article "Recovery from Addiction." He writes, "It is now well known that the repetition of rewarding behaviors produces changes in brain function and structure that facilitate habits and, for some, sustained compulsivity and addiction."

Dr. Kelly is saying that one reason we continue to act out is for the immediate reward of pleasure. But in order to find lasting sobriety, we must embrace the bigger reward.

We must give up what we want now for what we want most. And that is a reward of its own.

Paul confirms this principle, that God rewards those who make good decisions: "Whatever you do, work at it with all your heart, as working for the Lord, not for human masters, since you know that you will receive an inheritance from the Lord as a reward" (Col. 3:23–24).

Recovery Step: Enjoy the rewards of recovery—peace, freedom, and hope.

Weak Is Okay

MAY 27

The average man can bench press 135 pounds. That means that for every guy who can lift 270 pounds, there is another man who can barely lift a finger. But that's okay. Weak is okay.

It is in our weakness that we look to God's strength. David understood this when he penned, "[God] knows how we are formed, he remembers that we are dust" (Ps. 103:14).

Robin Williams, who fought addiction throughout his life, said wryly, "Reality is just a crutch for people who can't handle drugs."

Williams had a point. Where a lot of us get in trouble is not that we are weak; it's that we aren't okay with being weak. To find recovery, we must embrace weakness as a true gift from God. He has allowed us to be weak in order to recognize our need for him.

Step 1 says it right off the bat. It is the foundation for recovery: "We admitted we were powerless and that our lives had become unmanageable."

> **Recovery Step:** Take your weakness to God today. Admit your powerlessness over your struggles and lean into his strength.

1904 Olympics

MAY 28

The marathon at the 1904 Olympics in St. Louis was one for the ages. And Felix Carvajal, who came in fourth, was a crazy Cuban. To raise enough money to get to St. Louis he ran the entire length of Cuba. He arrived at the Olympics in dress clothing. And during the race, he stopped to take a nap.

What does the Bible say about running? Quite a bit, actually.

"Run with perseverance" (Heb. 12:1).

"I have finished the race" (2 Tim. 4:7).

But we also have this warning: "You were running a good race. Who cut in on you to keep you from obeying the truth?" (Gal. 5:7).

Recovery Step: The Christian life is a race. And recovery is a race. Actually, it's a marathon. And you cannot win unless you finish strong.

The Refuge of God

MAY 29

The Bible tells us the story of an amazing woman named Ruth. Her husband had died, so from that point on she faithfully cared for her mother-in-law. To do so, Ruth gladly left her homeland to live among people she did not know. This caught the eye of a wealthy man named Boaz, who blessed her greatly.

Boaz said to Ruth, "May the Lord repay you for what you have done. May you be richly rewarded by the Lord, the God of Israel, under whose wings you have come to take refuge" (Ruth 2:12).

For those who are willing to sacrifice their lives for the sake of others—as Ruth did—God offers a refuge of protection.

Josh Philpott of Founders Baptist Church in Spring, Texas, wrote an article posted on *Desiring God*. In "Troubled Heart, Take Refuge in God," Philpott wrote, "I realized that God's hand—his refuge—was protecting me from something greater: from *myself* and the *consequences of my own sin*."

God is in the business of protecting us from others—and from ourselves.

Recovery Step: Let your recovery take you places you never expected to go. Like Ruth, commit to being a blessing to someone who needs you today.

Planned Neglect

MAY 30

Sometimes it's what you don't do that makes the difference.

Someone asked a concert violinist how she became so skilled. She gave a two-word answer: "Planned neglect." She explained that she neglected everything that didn't contribute to her goal, which was to be a master violinist.

Successful recovery requires planned neglect. In order to grow in your recovery, you must learn to neglect certain people, movies, social media, and other distractions that take you off course.

I love the J. B. Phillips translation of Romans 12:2. "Don't let the world around you squeeze you into its own mold."

The "Denison version" is similar: "In order to be more Christ-like, you must embrace planned neglect."

Recovery Step: Identify one thing or person in your life that has become a detriment to your recovery. Then embrace the practice of planned neglect.

God Really Does This?

MAY 31

God does a lot of things. He creates. He saves. He redeems. He forgives. He protects. He leads. He provides. He overcomes. He heals.

But there's more. God does something else. The prophet Zephaniah declared, "The Lord your God is with you, the Mighty Warrior who saves. He will take great delight in you; in his love he will no longer rebuke you, but will rejoice over you with singing" (Zeph. 3:17).

Did you catch that? God rejoices over you with gladness!

This promise was given to all God's children, not just the super saints, faithful followers, perfect people, or best believers.

God looks at you—just as you are right now—and he rejoices. He doesn't wait until you get it all together, celebrate ten years of sobriety, or climb the tallest mountain. He rejoices over you right now. Let that sink in!

Recovery Step: There is nothing you can ever do to make God love you more. And nothing you have ever done has made him love you less. So rejoice in the One who rejoices in you!

JUNE

If you have to sneak around to do it, lie to cover it up, or delete it to avoid it being seen, then you probably shouldn't be doing it.

—Anonymous

The Saw

JUNE 1

A man had a firewood factory that employed hundreds of men. He paid them well and gave them specific directions on what to do, but their work was slow and unproductive. Eventually, he had no choice. He fired the men and purchased a circular saw powered by a gas engine. In one hour, the new saw accomplished more than the men had done in a week.

The man talked to his new saw. "How can you turn out so much work? Are you sharper than the saws my men were using before?"

The saw responded, "No, I am not sharper than the other saws. The difference is the gas engine. I have a stronger power behind me. I am productive because of the power that is working through me, not because my blade is stronger."

The man or woman who finds successful recovery doesn't do so because he or she has a better saw. It's all about the power within. The Bible calls that power the Holy Spirit.

Jesus promised his earliest followers, "You will receive power when the Holy Spirit comes on you" (Acts 1:8).

That's the secret. It's not the sharpness of the saw but the presence of the Spirit.

Recovery Step: Ask God to empower your saw through the filling and power of the Holy Spirit.

Quiet, Please!

JUNE 2

Mother Teresa: "God cannot be found in noise."

A 2006 study in the journal *Heart* found that silence can relieve tension in just two minutes.

In another study of 100 men and women who went on a silent retreat, Conor O'Shea found that simply being quiet before the Lord led each person to experience an increased awareness of who they were in the light of God.

I hear it a lot. "I'm fighting for recovery" or "I'm fighting for sexual purity."

Not only do I get that, but I often say it myself. And the premise that recovery is a fight, that it calls for hard work, is sound.

But we need to know when to tag out.

The Bible says, "The Lord will fight for you; you need only to be still" (Exod. 14:14).

Recovery Step: Now might be a good time for you to back off, sit down, look up, and wait on the Lord. Let him do in you what you cannot do yourself.

Slow! God at Work!

JUNE 3

A chicken and an elephant were locked in a cage together. The chicken turned to the elephant and said, "We need to set a few ground rules. First, let's not step on each other."

The chicken was looking at it from his point of view. Our chicken point of view affects our relationships with others. Our tendency is to want to straighten people out for our own benefit. This is especially true for those married to addicts.

If you think straightening people out is your job, I suggest you become a funeral director. That way, when you straighten them out, they will stay straightened out.

Only God can straighten people out. He is the great construction supervisor.

May we follow the Apostle Paul's advice: "Bear with each other and forgive one another if any of you has a grievance against someone. Forgive as the Lord forgave you" (Col. 3:13).

Recovery Step: Let up on those around you. You may be married to an addict. And while there is no excuse for his continued behavior (if he is not in recovery), you can't fix him. Only God is in the construction business.

Two Kinds of People

JUNE 4

There are two kinds of people in the world: those who enter a crowded room thinking, "Here I am!" and those who enter a room thinking, "Here you are!"

Which person are you?

This matters because our recovery is never complete until we help someone else with their recovery. We must learn to shift our focus from ourselves to others.

I love Francis Schaeffer's approach. He said, "If I have only an hour to spend with someone, I spend the first 55 minutes asking questions and finding out what it troubling them. Then I spend the last five minutes offering solutions."

That is so biblical. That is following the Lord's command: "Be quick to listen" (James 1:19).

In order to take your recovery to the next level, you need to be others-focused. Look for ways to help someone else grow in their recovery.

Recovery Step: Identify one person you can help with his or her recovery this week.

Bad Driver

JUNE 5

An unobservant driver made an illegal right turn onto another street. Exasperated, he turned to his young son in the passenger seat and said, "That was stupid! I just made an illegal right turn!"

His son offered encouragement. "Aw, dad, it's okay. The police car right behind us just did the same thing."

That boy clearly has the gift of encouragement.

Few things matter as much as encouragement. That's why the Bible says, "Encourage one another and build each other up" (1 Thess. 5:11).

Try that today. Encourage someone in their recovery. There are a squillion ways to do that. Pick one. In the process, your own recovery will move forward.

Recovery Step: There's enough negativity in this world. What we need is one more encourager. May that person be you.

Happy, Healthy, or Holy?

JUNE 6

One day, Jesus approached a crowd of people. Most of them were well. But Jesus noticed the lame man. He always notices the lame man. Jesus walked up to the man who had not walked in thirty-eight years and healed him.

But then the story took a strange turn. A brief time later, Jesus encountered the man in town, walking free of his limp. And then Jesus said to him, "Stop sinning or something worse may happen to you" (John 5:14).

"Something worse?" the man must have thought. "What could be worse than being crippled for thirty-eight years?"

A. W. Tozer said, "No man should desire to be happy who is not at the same time holy. He should spend his efforts in seeking to know and do the will of God, leaving to Christ the matter of how happy he should be."

God cares more about your character than your comfort.

Recovery Step: Stop sinning and acting out or something "worse" will happen. That's not my threat. It's God's promise.

Funny Sports Injuries

JUNE 7

My favorite sports are American football, basketball, and baseball. For the first two, I'm amazed at the athletes' ability to play through injuries—with baseball, not so much.

Here are just a few ways baseball players injured themselves badly enough to have to miss dozens of games.

- Sammy Sosa missed three weeks due to a back injury caused by sneezing too hard.
- Mariano Rivera threw his back out trying to tie his own shoes.
- John Smoltz burned himself by ironing his shirt while wearing it.
- Johnny Damon injured his back getting into a car.

I think the lesson here is that any of us can get hurt at just about any time. Applying that to daily life, Paul warned, "Be careful that you don't fall!" (1 Cor. 10:12).

> **Recovery Step:** It doesn't take much to get hurt. It doesn't take much to get into trouble. And it doesn't take much to be diligent—every day.

Shut the Door

JUNE 8

Before Jesus taught us what to pray, he taught us how to pray.

Jesus said, "But when you pray, go into your room and shut the door and pray to your Father who is in secret. And your Father who sees in secret will reward you" (Matt. 6:6 ESV).

Let me highlight three words you probably glossed over: "shut the door."

Sit with that for a moment. Our Lord is telling us that in order to have a productive prayer life, we will need to shut the door—to distractions, clutter, memories, unforgiveness, temptations, fantasies, and more.

Recovery Step: Christopher Columbus said, "By prevailing over all obstacles and distractions, one may unfailingly arrive at his chosen goal or destination." Every time you seek solitude with God, something will compete for your attention. The answer? Shut the door to any and all outside distractions.

Holy Habits

JUNE 9

Baseball Hall-of-Famer Al Kaline said, "You've got to get good habits of working hard so that when that play comes up during the regular season that you're able to complete it and do it the right way."

Your sobriety tomorrow will be determined by what you do today. It's all about developing the right habits.

Camel cigarettes knew this fifty years ago. They came out with an ad where they invited people to take the "30-day smoking test." They asked people to try Camel for thirty days, knowing that by that time they would be both loyal and addicted.

There was a man in the Bible who was the master of holy habits. His name was Daniel. When he was thrown into the lion's den, the king said, "May your God, whom you serve continually, rescue you!" (Dan. 6:16).

Do you want sobriety tomorrow? Then develop holy habits today—prayer, Scripture reading, worship, meetings, recovery work. The more you do the right thing today, the harder it will be to do the wrong thing tomorrow.

Recovery Step: Start developing one holy habit today in order to find real recovery tomorrow.

Dinosaurs

JUNE 10

Several visitors to the Chicago Museum of Natural History marveled at the site of the dinosaur bones. "How old are those bones?" they asked one of the workers.

"This particular dinosaur is three million, seven years, three months, and five days old," said the worker.

The visitors were impressed with the specificity of the man's answer. "That's a pretty exact age you gave us. How do you know this dinosaur is three million, seven years, three months, and five days old?"

"It's easy," replied the worker. "I started here seven years, three months, and five days ago. And on my first day on the job, they told me this dinosaur was three million years old."

Such truth is a relative thing. But truth that matters is not relative. That is especially the case with the Truth—the One who said, "You will know the truth, and the truth will set you free" (John 8:32).

Recovery Step: There is one truth you need to embrace and know personally—Jesus Christ.

Schizophrenia?

JUNE 11

Does God still speak to us? Thomas Szasz doesn't think so. He quipped, "If you talk to God, you are praying; if God talks to you, you have schizophrenia."

The Bible is clear. God has a history of speaking to us and through us. "Surely the sovereign Lord does nothing without revealing his plan to his servants the prophets" (Amos 3:7).

God speaks through his Word first and then through circumstances, other people, and the Holy Spirit. But make no mistake—God still speaks. The problem isn't that God is hiding from us; the problem is that we are not seeking him. He is speaking every day. Don't blame him because you're a poor listener.

You have to be weak enough to hear him. Hudson Taylor said, "God uses men who are weak and feeble enough to lean on him."

Recovery Step: Are you weak enough to hear the voice of God? If not, humble yourself before him today—for the sake of your recovery, family, and future.

Duck!

JUNE 12

On March 30, 1981, less than three months into his first term, President Ronald Reagan was shot by John Hinckley as he left a Washington, DC, hotel.

A few days later, Reagan explained what he did wrong. In his typical sense of humor, he told his wife, Nancy, "Honey, I forgot to duck."

Reagan borrowed that line from the great heavyweight boxing champion Jack Dempsey. After Dempsey's shocking knockout loss to Gene Tunney, he told his wife, "I forgot to duck."

Sometimes staying sober is that simple. We need to know when to duck. When you see an attractive person walking toward you at the mall, duck into a store. When you see a sexual scene unfolding on a television program, duck into the next room. When your buddies move the conversation to sexual topics, duck out of that conversation.

Jesus taught us to pray, "Lead us not into temptation, but deliver us from evil" (Matt. 6:13 ESV). Here's the *Readers Digest* version: "When temptation comes, know when to duck."

> **Recovery Step:** It's great to learn various recovery tools, attend meetings, and do therapy. But later today, when you see an incoming missile fired from the gun of relapse, learn to duck.

The Plane and the Farmhouse

JUNE 13

We always seem to want what we do not have.

A child on a farm sees a plane flying overhead and dreams of flying, while the pilot on the plane sees the farmhouse and dreams of returning home.

A man spends money he doesn't have in order to buy a new car while missing his first car (with no AC and only an AM radio) for the rest of his life.

We buy HD televisions as wide as our living room wall and then pull up a sixty-year-old black-and-white movie on an obscure movie channel.

We always seem to want what we do not have.

Welcome to the life of an addict. Yesterday's hit wore off overnight. Today's indulgence will leave us empty tomorrow. Nothing this world has to offer truly satisfies.

Recovery Step: If you want constant emptiness and hopelessness, stick with your addiction. But if you want true peace and joy, stick with "the Lord, the compassionate and gracious God, slow to anger, abounding in love and faithfulness" (Exod. 34:6).

Collect Calls

JUNE 14

Second Corinthians 10:5 tells us to "take captive every thought to make it obedient to Christ."

I encourage people to practice what I call the "three-second rule." When your eyes are triggered or an intrusive thought or memory invades your mind, move away from it within three seconds. Say a prayer, read a verse, make a call.

Let me illustrate. Back in the day, we had this thing in our house called a landline. It was a precursor to the modern cell phone. We called it a telephone. When someone wanted to contact us, they dialed our number, and this thing would ring. We'd pick up the receiver. And sometimes it would be what we called a "long distance call." This one cost money. We'd hear the voice of the "operator," who would ask us if we were willing to accept a call that was made "collect." In other words, once we knew who was trying to call us, we had about three seconds to decide if we were willing to pay to hear what they had to say.

Temptations always call collect. You will recognize the voice. And when you do, don't negotiate the price or ask what he or she wants. Just hang up—fast!

Recovery Step: The tempter has your number. He or she will come calling. And if you stay on the line, you will pay for that call, and it will cost you more than you can afford. So reject the call. Know when to hang up.

The Power of Three

JUNE 15

Jesus fed the 5,000. He trained the seventy. He discipled the twelve. But he put far more energy into the three—Peter, James, and John.

Jesus took these three to the Mount of Transfiguration. For the healing of Peter's mother-in-law, he took the three. When he raised Jairus's daughter to life, the three were there. And while the twelve accompanied him to the Garden of Gethsemane, he took the three "a little farther" (Matt. 26:39) for an intimate time of prayer.

Pay attention to your group of three.

In recovery, you need an accountability partner, a support group, and a larger community. But there is no substitute for a very tight group of about three others (same sex) who know your story, believe in you, and are happy to go "a little farther" than the rest.

Recovery Step: Make a list of three people who can be in your inner circle.

It's Not Your Fight!

JUNE 16

In the Civil War, 620,000 lives were lost, equal to all other American wars combined. The carnage ended on April 9, 1865, at Appomattox, Virginia, when General Robert E. Lee surrendered his 28,000 troops. Then it was up to President Lincoln to decide the fate of the soldiers on both sides. Lincoln chose peace and reconciliation. He did for the South what they could not do for themselves.

There was a king in the Bible named Jehoshaphat. His army faced a formidable enemy, one he knew they could not conquer. The king turned to God who issued a promise for the ages.

"You will not have to fight this battle" (2 Chron. 20:17).

Andrew Murray said it like this: "God is ready to assume full responsibility for the life wholly yielded to him."

The battle for sobriety is not your battle to win. Victory is found only through surrender to your Higher Power who has all strength.

Recovery Step: Surrender to the only One strong enough to win the battle.

Tag Teams

JUNE 17

According to many professional wrestling experts, the greatest wrestling tag team of all time was the Road Warriors, known individually as Animal and Hawk. From 1983 to 2014, this ruthless tag team won dozens of titles, including the NWA World Championship three times. (And don't tell me wrestling is fake!)

Here's how they did it. When Animal got into trouble, Hawk would cheat, pull someone's hair, and utilize a foreign object seen by every person in the arena other than the referee. And when Hawk was in trouble, Animal would do the same.

The Bible says, "Two are better than one" (Eccles. 4:9). You need a tag team partner in recovery.

There will be times when you need to tag out. In the heat of the battle, in the midst of the temptation, you need help. That is when you make a call. You reach out for help. And with that person's help, you can win another match.

Recovery Step: Get a tag team partner. That will be key to your success.

The First Cabinet

JUNE 18

It happened in 1791. Thomas Jefferson, Alexander Hamilton, Henry Knox, and Edmund Randolph met with George Washington at his home in Philadelphia. This was the first official cabinet meeting for the new republic.

Wouldn't you love to have been a fly on the wall for that historic gathering?

Together, those five men laid out the next steps for the fledgling country. But it took Washington fifteen years—from the signing of the Declaration of Independence to this meeting—to gather a cabinet. He chose carefully.

The power of a small group cannot be overstated. When Jesus selected his own cabinet—the twelve disciples—the Holy Spirit was sure to remind three Gospel writers to include that in their story (Matt. 10, Mark 3, Luke 6).

Recovery Step: You need a group in your corner. Select them carefully.

John Belushi

JUNE 19

Isolation is both a trigger and a fear. Being alone is a threat to our recovery since we thrive on connection, which is the opposite of addiction.

Actor John Belushi's final words were quite telling. Shortly before his death in 1982, he said, "Just don't leave me alone."

No one wants to be left alone.

Fortunately, we serve a God who offers connection. "Because of the Lord's great love we are not consumed, for his compassions never fail. They are new every morning; great is your faithfulness. I say to myself, 'The Lord is my portion; therefore I will wait for him'" (Lam. 3:22–24).

Let me share the three Es of connection. With the right connection with others, we find:

- Enlightenment
- Encouragement
- Example

Remember, isolation from God and others is a choice, not a condition. You can always choose connection. You must always choose connection.

Recovery Step: Connect with God and one other person in recovery today.

The South Pole

JUNE 20

The year was 1911. The South Pole was not the vacation paradise it is today. But a Norwegian explorer named Roald Amundsen changed all that when he set out to become the first person to reach the South Pole. While assembling his team, Amundsen chose expert skiers and dog handlers. His strategy was simple. The dogs would do most of the work as they pulled the group 15 to 20 miles a day. Rather than rely on their own strength, they would rely on the strength of the dogs. It worked, and Amundsen became the first person to reach the South Pole.

The road to recovery is one of exploration. None of us got it right the first time. And as long as we sought sobriety in our own strength, we found no recovery at all.

The key to lasting recovery is surrender to our Higher Power. As Amundsen relied on the strength of his dogs, we must rely on the strength of our God.

King David wrote, "The Lord is the strength of my life; of whom shall I be afraid?" (Ps. 27:1 NKJV).

Alexander MacLaren nailed it: "Only he who can say, 'The Lord is the strength of my life' can say, 'Of whom shall I be afraid?'"

Recovery Step: You aren't strong enough to find recovery on your own. Turn your life and will over to the care of God. Rely only on him, or you'll never reach your Promised Land.

A Single Punch

JUNE 21

On November 5, 1994, Michael Moorer, the undefeated heavyweight champion of the world, stepped into the ring against forty-five-year-old George Foreman who had not won a meaningful fight in nearly twenty years. Moorer led on all three judges' cards entering the final round. Then Foreman landed a single, devastating punch. Moorer went down. He would not get up.

Like Michael Moorer, you can be ahead on points in recovery and still go down with a single blow.

Jesus's close friend Peter serves as an astounding example.

> *When seizing him, they led him away and took him into the house of the high priest. Peter followed at a distance. And when some there had kindled a fire in the middle of the courtyard and had sat down together, Peter sat down with them. A servant girl saw him seated there in the firelight. She looked closely at him and said, "This man was with him." But he denied it. "Woman, I don't know him."*
>
> —Luke 22:54

Recovery Step: Your addiction can bring you down with a single punch. So with every tool available and with every ounce of energy you have, keep fighting until the final bell rings.

Set Your Heart

JUNE 22

"Ezra had set his heart to study the Law of the Lord, and to do it and to teach his statutes and rules in Israel" (Ezra 7:10 ESV).

This verse highlights Ezra's dedication to God's Word and his commitment to teaching and upholding the Law.

But there's more. Catch these five words: "Ezra had set his heart."

Ezra didn't wait for the feeling to wash over him. He didn't wait for an outside motivation to rise up and pull him in. Ezra determined the direction of his heart. He determined to chase after the person of God and the Word of God, whether he always felt like it or not.

Ezra decided to become a thermostat instead of a thermometer. Rather than waiting on his heart to seek God, Ezra set his heart.

Recovery Step: If you put off sobriety until your heart becomes emotionally captivated, you may be waiting a while. Quit responding to what your heart wants and start doing what your heart needs. Set your heart toward recovery.

From the Lion to the Bear

JUNE 23

Do you ever overcome one obstacle only to find the next one waiting for you?

The prophet Amos wrote, "It will be as though a man fled from a lion only to meet a bear" (Amos 5:19).

In life, it's always a good thing to run from the nearest lion. But know this: That is not the end of the journey. The bear is waiting to make a personal introduction.

Michael Phelps said, "There will be obstacles. There will be doubters. There will be mistakes. But with hard work, . . . there are no limits."

I have experienced all three—obstacles, doubters, and mistakes. I'd love to say I prayed them away or that I found some mystical way to overcome each one. But the truth is that it has taken years of hard work to overcome some of those obstacles, doubters, and mistakes.

Name your obstacle, doubter, or mistake. Then take them to God. Seek his face for each one. Then commit to the hard work of recovery.

Recovery Step: Commit to doing the hard work.

Wesley's Last Words

JUNE 24

Not long ago, my wife, Beth, and I watched a television show where viewers were allowed to phone in their vote to determine how that episode would end. And that's how it is in life. We don't get to choose how we start, but we do get to choose how we end.

When John Wesley lay on his deathbed, he reflected on his life. Living from 1703 to 1791, Wesley traveled 250,000 miles by horseback and preached 40,000 sermons. On his last night on earth, he summoned his family to his bedside and spoke his final words.

"The best of all is, God is with us! The best of all is, God is with us."

You didn't choose the struggles of your life. And you can't do anything to go back and change the past. The fact is, you can't really change the future. But you have this promise: No matter how hard the journey, you will not walk alone.

When the journey ends, Jesus said that some "will go away to eternal punishment, but the righteous to eternal life" (Matt. 25:46). Those paths will have long since been paved before that day comes. The battles will not be easy, but one thing is sure: You need not walk alone.

Recovery Step: Settle your relationship with God today. Nothing matters more than his presence in your life. Wesley had it right. "The best of all is, God is with us. The best of all is, God is with us."

How the Brain Works

JUNE 25

Why do addicts become addicts? What happens on a physiological level?

Substances and behaviors of abuse act directly on the reward center of the brain to deliver their high. That involves speedy and intense release of the neurotransmitter dopamine. Addictive behaviors become a shortcut to reward that over time can have a high cost to physical and mental health. Nevertheless, the outsized sensation of reward makes a powerful case for repetition. And through pathways of nerve connection to other areas of the brain, the response weakens activity of the brain's decision-making center in the prefrontal cortex.

As a result of the compulsion, we often choose "to enjoy the fleeting pleasures of sin" (Heb. 11:25).

What's the answer? How do you get off the crazy train?

The answer is found in Step 2. "We came to recognize that a Power greater than ourselves could restore us to sanity."

Recovery Step: You need to embrace two basic truths if you are to become sober: (1) without God, you can't, and (2) without you, God won't.

The Best Timber

JUNE 26

A hiker crossed paths with a farmer who was hiking up a mountain with an ax in his hand. The hiker asked the farmer why he had the ax, and the farmer answered, "I'm climbing the mountain with an ax to cut up some timber because I'm making a wagon."

The hiker replied, "But look around you. There are plenty of trees right here. Why are you climbing the mountain to cut wood?"

The farmer explained, "I need the strongest wood I can find. That kind of wood only grows in the mountain where it has withstood the strongest storms."

God toughens us up through life's greatest storms. When you are tempted to lament your trauma or abuse, remember that God will bless you, not despite your past but because of it. Thank him that you are storm-tested.

> **Recovery Step:** The Bible says, "He brings the clouds . . . to water his earth and show his love" (Job 37:13). Sometimes this "watering" takes the form of enormous storms. Are you in a storm right now? As hard as it will be to do, thank God that when the sun comes out, you'll be better for having passed through the storm.

Danger, Will Robinson

JUNE 27

It was a classic TV hit in the early days of sci-fi shows. Though it wasn't on for long, *Lost in Space* captured a loyal audience from 1965 to 1968. Most viewers will remember the iconic line from the robot to the young boy on the show: "Danger, Will Robinson!"

You may be surprised to know that this line was only found in one of the eighty-nine episodes. Still, it is the most memorable line from the entire series.

God gave a similar warning to the first family. Knowing that Cain was not where he needed to be spiritually, the Lord told him, "Sin is crouching at your door" (Gen. 4:7).

Cain killed his brother the next day.

Recovery Step: Never forget the presence of sin crouching at your door. Relapse is always a clear and present danger.

Promises, Promises

JUNE 28

We all love the promises of God. In the Bible, there are 7,500 of them, promises such as:

- Peace
- Heaven
- Joy
- Wisdom
- Connection

Here's another one from the lips of Jesus. "In this world you will have trouble" (John 16:33).

Wait a minute! I didn't sign up for that! Give me the promises about prosperity and peace, happiness and health, fun and good times. But trouble? Are you kidding me, Jesus?

There's a line in the Serenity Prayer that most of us have never prayed: "Living one day at a time; enjoying one moment at a time; accepting hardship as the pathway to peace."

Yes, the road to peace is often paved with bricks made out of hardships. In the Christian life, trouble is not a possibility; it is a promise.

Recovery Step: Ten percent of recovery is what happens to you. The other 90 percent is how you react.

15 Rounds

JUNE 29

The third Ali-Frazier fight was one for the ages. The "Thrilla in Manila" was a brutal contest fought in 1975 toward the end of each fighter's career. Ali emerged the winner when Frazier was unable to answer the bell for the fifteenth round.

Like that epic battle, to win in recovery you must be able to go the distance. And the only way to do that is to have a spiritual connection with the God of the universe who said, "I live in a high and holy place" (Isa. 57:15).

J. C. Ryle summed it up perfectly. "There is no holiness without a warfare."

Are you willing to step into the ring against the strongest foe you will ever face—your addiction? If you are willing to enter the ring, there is good news. You will have the best corner man ever. God will be there with you through every round, every punch to the gut, and every knockdown. But you must be willing to go the distance.

Benjamin Alire Sáenz said of addictions, "If you can quit for a day, you can quit for a lifetime." He is right. The victory can be yours, one day and one round at a time.

Recovery Step: When you sign on for recovery, you step into life's toughest battle. But it is a battle you can win, one round at a time.

The Right Time

JUNE 30

"Christ came at just the right time" (Rom. 5:6 NLT).

Timing is everything. Yogi Berra said, "You don't have to swing hard to hit a home run. If you got the timing, it'll go." And Buzz Aldrin said, "Timing has always been a key element in my life. I have been blessed to have been in the right place at the right time."

Let's apply that to recovery. How does Jesus come "at just the right time"? I can only speak for myself. Upon my discovery, I found the right therapist at just the right time. I did my disclosure at just the right time. I found the right 12-Step group, sponsor, and mentors—all at just the right time.

We launched our ministry at just the right time. And every step of the way, we have seen God show up at just the right time.

Recovery Step: Learn to not only trust God but to trust God's timing. What was true 2,000 years ago is still true today. Jesus will come "at just the right time."

JULY

My own experience about all the blessings I've had in my life is that the more I give away, the more that comes back.

—Ken Blanchard

A Story of Survival

JULY 1

In July 2018, Angela Hernandez was driving near Bug Sur on Highway 1, headed to Southern California in her SUV, when a small animal crossed the road. Hernandez swerved to miss it and in doing so shot her SUV off the road and over a cliff, tumbling 200 feet to a desolate, rocky beach.

She had a brain hemorrhage, fractured ribs, broken collar bone, ruptured blood vessels in both eyes, and a collapsed lung, but she didn't die. When Angela came to, water lapped over her knees. She broke her window and crawled out the window, swam to the beach, and passed out.

When she awoke, she saw that there was no one in sight. She walked for days until spotted by hikers who descended to her by rope and saved Angela Hernandez.

Angela Hernandez is an example of endurance and determination—the kind that leads to sustained recovery.

Recovery Step: "Not only so, but we also glory in our sufferings, because we know that suffering produces perseverance; perseverance, character; and character, hope" (Rom. 5:3–4).

Underwater Somersaults

JULY 2

Underwater somersaulting is not yet an official Olympic sport. But that never stopped Marta Fernandez Perez from setting a world record in 2001 when she completed twenty-eight backward somersaults underwater—on one breath.

How did Marta come to be the queen of underwater somersaults? I'm not sure, but I'm going to guess that she didn't achieve this incredible feat the first time she hit the pool. Like all success stories, she probably failed before she succeeded.

Robert F. Kennedy said, "Only those who dare to fail greatly can ever achieve greatly."

Paul said it like this: "Whatever you do, do it all for the glory of God" (1 Cor. 10:31).

Recovery Step: I've never known anyone who got recovery right the first time. I doubt you'll be the first. And that's okay. Go all in. Risk it all. Why? Because that is the only way you'll get where you want to be.

Too Soon to Quit

JULY 3

In recovery, the measure of success is not whether you ever have a slip or relapse but how you respond. Don't misunderstand me; you should never have another slip or relapse. But if you do, keep this verse close by: "For though the righteous fall seven times, they rise again, but the wicked stumble when calamity strikes" (Prov. 24:16).

Did you catch that? "The righteous fall."

Quit focusing on the end game and start looking to the next twenty-four hours. In recovery, you will find milestones but no finish line.

I don't know most of you who are reading this right now, but I do know two things about you:

- It's too soon to quit.
- It's too late to stop.

Recovery Step: It's too soon to quit and too late to stop pushing forward. So just take one step today in the right direction.

1776

JULY 4

On July 4, 1776, the Second Continental Congress unanimously adopted the Declaration of Independence, severing the thirteen American colonies' political ties to Great Britain. The decree for freedom was actually made on July 2 with the passing of the Lee Resolution that called for separation from the British Crown, foreign alliances, and a plan for confederation. However, the Declaration was not signed until July 4.

Mankind has always treasured freedom. Go to any recovery meeting and you'll hear men and women talk about it. They want freedom—from their addictions, hurts, habits, and hang-ups.

God is pro-freedom. "Now the Lord is the Spirit, and where the Spirit of the Lord is, there is freedom" (2 Cor. 3:17).

If you want freedom, chase after it. Seek it. Pray for it. Work for it. Never forget, freedom is a choice more than a condition.

Recovery Step: "We must be free not because we claim freedom, but because we practice it" (William Faulkner).

The First YouTube Video

JULY 5

The first YouTube video was an eighteen-second clip called "Me at the Zoo." It was uploaded by the site's cofounder, Jawed Karim, on April 23, 2005. The video was first recorded by Karim's high school friend, Yakov Lapitsky, at the San Diego Zoo, featuring Karim in front of the elephant habitat.

Major achievements often evolve from humble beginnings.

The same is true of recovery. The Bible warns us to not "despise the day of small things" (Zech. 4:10).

Every person who has experienced years of solid recovery can remember attending their first meeting, working the 1st Step, and putting in the early work of recovery. You can't secure long-term recovery in a day, but you can start it in a day.

Recovery Step: The best time to get serious about recovery was last year. The second best time is right now.

Make a Wish

JULY 6

Ever wonder how the Make-a-Wish thing got started?

In 1980, doctors diagnosed Chris, age seven, with leukemia. He wanted to be a motorcycle police officer when he grew up. A friend of his family spoke to a member of the Arizona Highway Patrol, and within a few days, several officers came by to visit Chris.

After the meeting, the officers wanted to do more. They arranged for Chris to ride on a police helicopter and in a police car. They got him a police uniform and replaced his wheelchair with a battery-powered motorcycle. When he died, he was given full police honors.

This was the spark of the Make-a-Wish Foundation.

Second Thessalonians 1:11 says, "We constantly pray for you, that our God may make you worthy of his calling, and that by his power he may bring to fruition your every desire for goodness and your every deed prompted by faith."

Recovery starts with a wish. When put to action, Make-a-Wish becomes a foundation for a lifetime of recovery.

Recovery Step: State your wish for sobriety today. Then do the things that help that wish come true.

Enough

JULY 7

Saving Private Ryan may be the greatest war movie ever produced. The film traces a mission to bring Private James Ryan home after his three brothers were all killed in battle. Under the command of Captain Miller, a small group of soldiers went through hell to rescue Private Ryan. Most of the others, including Captain Miller, were killed in the process.

Decades later, an elderly James Ryan visited Captain Miller's grave at the cemetery in Normandy. Standing over Miller's grave, Ryan said, "I tried to live my life the best that I could. I hope that was enough."

Let those five words sink in: "I hope that was enough."

There is no way to know that what you have done was enough. You can't go back and do anything about the past, but starting today, you can live a life of integrity. Solomon said, "Whoever walks in integrity walks securely, but whoever takes crooked paths will be found out" (Prov. 10:9).

If you want to honor those who have helped you through the battle, that is exactly what you need to do. Live a life of integrity. That will be enough.

Recovery Step: Starting today, live a life that honors God.

The Problem with Lucy

JULY 8

When I want deep philosophical thought, I turn to . . . Charlie Brown.

I love the recurring theme of *Peanuts* between Charlie Brown and Lucy, who reminds Charlie that he is the problem. Charlie asks what he can do about that. Lucy responds that her job is not to give prescriptions but to simply point out the problem.

We all have at least one Lucy in our lives, someone who sees their role in life as that of pointing out our problems—no solutions, just condemnation.

For each of us, the Bible offers encouragement.

"So do not fear, for I am with you; do not be dismayed, for I am your God. I will strengthen you and help you; I will uphold you with my righteous right hand" (Isa. 41:10).

You already know your shortcomings. Now it's time to turn to the One who can do something about it.

Recovery Step: Surrender to the God of all encouragement.

The Perfect Fit

JULY 9

One night at the dinner table, a wife asked her husband, "Why is it that you always give me the smaller piece of steak now? When we first got married, you always cut me the larger piece of the streak. You don't love me anymore!"

"Not at all," said her husband.

"Then why do you take the larger piece of steak now?"

He explained, "Because you're a better cook now."

There is an interesting word in the Bible about marriage. God said the woman was created to be a "fit" for her husband (Gen. 2:18 ESV).

That describes every good marriage I know. The man and woman may not make much sense on their own, but together, they "fit."

Recovery Step: If you're married, celebrate that fact. Your imperfect spouse married an imperfect spouse (you) because together, you fit.

Who Has the Most Sobriety?

JULY 10

The next time you attend a recovery meeting, I can tell you how to tell who in that group has the most sobriety. It will be the person who got up earliest that morning.

Sobriety is truly a one-day-at-a-time proposition.

Charles Schulz said it like this: "Life is like an ice cream cone, you have to lick it one day at a time."

You can only scale Mount Recovery one step at a time. It's the next meeting, the next call, the next prayer. It's about diverting your eyes, saying the Serenity Prayer, changing the channel. Recovery is the accumulation of a whole bunch of small things done well.

I read somewhere that "the cow jumped over the moon." Maybe cows can do that. I can't. I must be content with small steps, not giant leaps.

Recovery Step: "Therefore do not worry about tomorrow, for tomorrow will worry about itself" (Matt. 6:34). Recovery can be yours—one step at a time.

The Price of a Babe Ruth Bat

JULY 11

On May 14, 2020, a bat once swung by Babe Ruth sold for $930,000. His 1920 jersey sold for $4.4 million, and his 1927 World Series ring sold for $2.1 million.

Joe DiMaggio's hand-written journal sold for $1.5 million.

A copy of the United States Constitution once held by George Washington sold for $9.8 million, while his pistols sold for $2 million.

President John F. Kennedy's watch sold for $350,000, his golf clubs sold for $772,000, and his Rolex watch given to him by Marilyn Monroe in 1962 sold for $120,000.

Here's the lesson. The value of an object is found in its owner. That is especially true with followers of Christ. The Bible says, "You were bought at a price; do not become slaves of human beings" (1 Cor. 7:23).

Recovery Step: Your value is not dependent on the success of your recovery, but on the price Jesus paid on the cross. Rejoice in that!

P + P = A

JULY 12

I was the strange guy who enjoyed algebra in high school. I've always loved mathematics and formulas. So here's a formula for you. What does it mean?

P + P = A

Your wait is over. Those three letters represent the following: Problem + Powerlessness = Addiction.

You can have a problem without it being an addiction. And you can be powerless over something without it being a problem. But when you put the two together—problem and powerlessness—well, you have an addiction.

Your unwanted sexual behavior is the problem. The fact that you haven't been able to overcome this compulsion for a sustained period of time means you are powerless. But there is hope.

"Power belongs to you, God" (Ps. 62:11). You can beat this addiction, but you can't do it on your own.

Recovery Step: Claim the only Power that can overcome your addiction.

Connecting the Dots

JULY 13

God has given us three kinds of sight; we need all three.

- Foresight: a vision for what can be
- Insight: an understanding of what has come
- Hindsight: learning from our past

Let's talk about that last one—hindsight. Sometimes our past is our best teacher.

During his commencement address at Stanford University, Steve Jobs said, "You can't connect the dots looking forward; you can only connect them looking backwards."

The Bible encourages us, "Remember the days of old, consider the generations long past. Ask your father and he will tell you, your elders, and they will explain to you" (Deut. 32:7).

Recovery Step: Think back over your past wins, losses, and draws. Ask God to give you one lesson from your past that can pave the way for a better tomorrow.

Restitution

JULY 14

Restitution: It's something we don't talk about much, and we do it even less. But restitution is a key to recovery. Restitution is a biblical word for making amends. And the concept is rooted in the Law of Moses.

One of the earliest writings of the Law includes a passage on making restitution.

"[They] must confess the sin they have committed. They must make full restitution for the wrong they have done, add a fifth of the value to it and give it all to the person they have wronged" (Num. 5:7).

God has provided clear steps for those who have violated others. Those steps include admitting the wrong things we have done and providing restitution whenever possible. If we follow these simple steps, we will make significant progress toward recovery.

There are three kinds of amends—direct, indirect, and living—and they all count. In recovery, we seek to make things right. In the process, God makes us right.

Recovery Step: Ask God to bring to mind a person you need to make amends or restitution with. Then pray about what kind of amends you need to make—direct, indirect, or living.

It's How We Help

JULY 15

The 12th Step tells us to help others find recovery. Ben Franklin tells us how: "Tell me and I forget, teach me and I may remember, involve me and I learn."

In order to secure our own recovery, we must help others secure theirs. We do that by example, not lectures. It is by walking beside those who are new to recovery that we offer our best. What they need is not our wisdom as much as our lives.

The psalmist wrote, "One generation commends your works to another" (Ps. 145:4).

In the days of the Old Testament, multiple generations of the same family lived together. No one ever moved out until they moved up. Grandpa instructed grandson by his personal example. And that is how recovery works.

Your task is to find someone who has less recovery than you. Then resist the temptation to tell them everything you know. Instead, walk beside them. Give them your life, not your great intellect.

Recovery Step: Walk beside someone new to recovery this week.

Strawberry Fields Forever

JULY 16

In 1967, The Beatles released one of their most confusing hits, *Strawberry Fields*. John Lennon was inspired to write the words based on his childhood memories of playing in the garden of Strawberry Field, which was a children's home in Liverpool. It required five weeks of recording, spread over 45 hours, for the iconic rock group to create the product that would rocket to the top of the charts.

The song is all about escapism. During the unsettled times of the 1960s, listeners would be reminded of the carefree childhood they had left behind, and the desire to return to the "Strawberry Fields" of their youth.

The Beatles would release three versions of *Strawberry Fields,* with one earning recognition as the seventh ranked song of all time on *Rolling Stone*'s "500 Greatest Songs of All Time." Jesus had his own version.

"But Jesus often withdrew to lonely places and prayed" (Luke 5:16).

Recovery Step: Find a solitary place to pray. Find your own Strawberry Fields - forever.

Progress, Not Perfection

JULY 17

Let me say up front that there is no license for acting out. It is never right, and it should never happen. Once you enter recovery, it is possible to never again view porn, masturbate, or act out. And God's intended will is that you never break your sobriety—ever.

And for many, this will be the case. But hear this: Recovery is about progress, not perfection. Nobody works their recovery perfectly. And if you do have a slip, remember . . . it's about progress, not perfection.

Paul told the local church, "I don't mean to say that I have already achieved these things or that I have already reached perfection. But I press on to possess that perfection for which Christ Jesus first possessed me" (Phil. 3:12 NLT).

Perfection is out of reach. Progress is not.

Plato warned us, "Never discourage anyone . . . who continually makes progress, no matter how slow."

Recovery Step: Encourage someone who is struggling to stay in the battle for sobriety. If they aren't perfect, try to remember two things: God's not done with them yet, and you probably aren't perfect either.

Three Stages of Relapse

JULY 18

Relapses are the predictable outcome of a series of poor choices. A relapse is never an event but rather a process. Relapses come in three phases:

- Emotional relapse
- Mental relapse
- Physical relapse

Don't focus too much on the physical part of relapse, the actual acting out behavior. Focus more on how you get to that point. Give greater attention to what is going on emotionally and mentally. When those areas are healthy, the chances of physical relapse drop dramatically.

Too many of us play with fire. We relapse in our thought life, thinking we can withstand the temptation we bring on ourselves.

Paul offered this bit of warning: "So, if you think you are standing firm, be careful that you don't fall!" (1 Cor. 10:12). In other words, rather than fighting temptation, we should avoid it in the first place whenever possible.

Recovery Step: Avoid the first stages of relapse.

Overcoming Stupid

JULY 19

William Shatner said, "I'm gonna reveal something to you that's going to come as a shock: If you're a stupid young man, you're usually a stupid old man. Most people, including myself, keep repeating the same mistakes."

Solomon said it like this: "As a dog returns to its vomit, so fools repeat their folly" (Prov. 26:11).

As addicts, we almost invariably repeat the patterns of the past. Our old problems revisit us again and again. When we relax in our recovery program, we are setting ourselves up for a relapse into our old lifestyle. Only through perseverance will we be able to overcome our dependency.

Legendary University of Texas Coach Darrell Royal said, "I try not to make the same mistakes today that I made yesterday."

What is the difference between a dog who returns to its vomit and an addict who returns to their habit? Answer: the dog's actions make more sense.

Recovery Step: Get off the crazy cycle of addiction. Take the necessary steps of recovery, one day at a time, starting today.

Time to Journal

JULY 20

Dr. Catherine Cox did a thorough study of 301 of history's greatest geniuses. She discovered one common denominator among them. All of them recorded their thoughts, feelings, ideas, and insights.

Today, we call it journaling.

Author Bailey Balfour suggests five reasons to journal.

- Journaling reduces stress.
- It improves immune function.
- It keeps the memory sharp.
- It boosts our mood.
- It strengthens our emotional functions.

Recovery Step: The prophet Habakkuk said, "Write the vision, make it plain on tablets, so he may run who reads it" (Hab. 2:2 ESV). In other words, journal!

Working the 4th Step

JULY 21

Jason Wahler, founder of Widespread Recovery, stated, "The addiction is but a symptom of a spiritual disease. The real problem is in character flaws that need to be faced and overcome. This requires one thing—total honesty."

Therein lies the rub: total honesty. That is what the 4th Step is all about. That is what recovery is all about. Most of us wished we could have avoided taking a personal inventory. It's normal to hide from personal examination. But in our hearts we knew that day would come when we would have to face the truth about ourselves.

The Bible warns of a day when no one can hide. "And I saw the dead, great and small, standing before the throne, and books were opened. Another book was opened, which is the book of life. The dead were judged according to what they had done as recorded in the books" (Rev. 20:12).

It is best to do our inventory now so we will be ready for the big one to come. The 4th Step is just nine words: "Made a searching and fearless moral inventory of ourselves." But those are nine powerful words.

Recovery Step: If you haven't already done so, you need to work on the 4th Step under the guidance of your sponsor.

It's Possible

JULY 22

Chris Norton broke his neck while playing college football. He was given a 3 percent chance of ever moving again. Norton didn't get sad; he got mad. After months of hard work, he wiggled a toe. Eventually, he was able to get up out of his wheelchair and walk 7 feet—down the wedding aisle.

"Nothing will be impossible with God" (Luke 1:37 ESV).

Let's talk about that word—*nothing.*

This is God's message:

- To the addict: Sobriety is possible.
- To the spouse: Healing is possible.
- To the couple: Reconciliation is possible.

Either nothing will be impossible with God or the entire Bible is called into question. That doesn't mean these enormous challenges will be easy, but it does mean they are possible.

Recovery Step: Move every challenge in your life into the category of "possible."

Presumptions

JULY 23

A new CEO demanded hard work from his employees. One day, he saw a guy standing by the food table doing nothing. He yelled, "You're fired! Get out of here!"

Then he turned to one of the other men and said, "Smith, see what happens to slackers? Tell me in your own words what just happened!"

Smith: "Well, sir, you just fired the pizza delivery guy."

Moses spoke of a day when "all the people shall hear and fear and not act presumptuously again" (Deut. 17:13 ESV).

Presumption gets us into trouble every time. Now apply that to recovery. Let me say it with five words: Don't judge another person's recovery.

Every person in recovery has experienced different (a) trauma, (b) abuse, (c) isolation, (d) circumstances, and (e) triggers.

The answer: When you see someone else struggling, don't presume. Pray.

Recovery Step: Put presumptions of other people on the top shelf and then throw away your ladder.

Vodka and the Holy Spirit

JULY 24

"Trust me, you can dance." —Vodka

Alcohol has that effect on people. With a few drinks, the alcohol takes over, and you become someone different.

That explains Ephesians 5:18. Paul wrote, "Do not get drunk on wine, which leads to debauchery. Instead, be filled with the Holy Spirit."

Why did Paul draw a correlation between drunkenness and being filled with the Spirit? Because when you are filled with the Spirit, you become someone different.

Reinhard Bonnke wrote, "The less Holy Spirit we have, the more cake and coffee we need to keep the church going."

Many of us do recovery the same way. We rely on just about anything except the Holy Spirit.

Recovery Step: Empty yourself and receive the filling of the Holy Spirit today. Your recovery depends on it.

Impossible!

JULY 25

One day in the late 1800s, a religious leader was asked his opinion on the possibility of flight. "Nonsense!" he said. "We'll never fly!"

The name of the religious leader was Bishop Wright. The names of his two boys were Orville and Wilbur. Perhaps you've heard of them.

What seems impossible is often made possible.

An angel told Mary, still a virgin, that she would give birth to a really important son. When Mary questioned the plausibility of such an occurrence, the angel assured her, "Nothing will be impossible with God" (Luke 1:37 ESV).

What seems impossible is often made possible.

What does this mean for recovery? Everything.

Recovery Step: Stop right now and say it with me. What seems impossible is often made possible.

Dr. Denton Cooley

JULY 26

In 1969, Dr. Denton Cooley performed the world's first successful heart transplant. His iconic career was marked by unmatched recognition over five decades of groundbreaking work. As an aside, he performed heart surgery on my dad, saving his life in 1960.

Dr. Cooley was not shy about his success. Once appearing as an expert witness in a major trial, Cooley was asked by the lawyer if he considered himself the best heart surgeon in the world. When he answered in the affirmative, the attorney asked him, "Don't you think that's being rather immodest?"

"Perhaps," Cooley responded, "but remember, I'm under oath."

Dr. Cooley has more things named after him than some Presidents. But even the strong can struggle. Sadly, in 1988 at the age of sixty-eight following a series of bad investments, the greatest heart surgeon in the world filed for bankruptcy.

We all fail at times. But that's okay because it is when we are down that we tend to look up.

Recovery Step: "The Lord helps the fallen and lifts those bent beneath their loads" (Ps. 145:14 NLT). Let him lift you now.

"Rabbit"

JULY 27

"Rabbit" Maranville was a 5'3" baseball player born in 1891. He made it to the big leagues when he was twenty-one. Though just a career .258 hitter, "Rabbit" stuck it out for twenty-three years. While bouncing among five teams—the Braves, Pirates, Cubs, Dodgers, and Cardinals—"Rabbit" could do one thing well. He could run. And he ran faster than anyone else.

But alcohol nearly ended his life as a young player. Then one night in 1927, "Rabbit" gave his life to his Higher Power. Christ changed his life, and "Rabbit" never took another drink.

But choices have consequences. In 1954, "Rabbit" died from the effects of years of alcohol abuse. Two weeks later, he was elected to the Baseball Hall of Fame.

But again, choices have consequences. Paul said it like this: "The wages of sin is death" (Rom. 6:23).

In the movie *The Number 23*, Jim Carrey's character said, "There's no such thing as destiny. There are only different choices."

Recovery Step: Tomorrow's destiny is in your hands today. You can't see your destiny, but you can create it—one choice at a time.

The Road Less Traveled

JULY 28

You are probably familiar with Robert Frost's famous poem "The Road Not Taken" where he depicts a person facing a dilemma. He has two possible pathways to choose from—one that is frequently traveled and one that is rarely taken. In the poem, the person chooses the road less traveled.

For the addict, the road less traveled is Recovery Boulevard. Some studies indicate that only 10 percent of addicts choose to do any serious recovery work. Most live in their addiction making only casual, infrequent attempts to find their way out.

Many want to be recovered. They want the destination but not the journey. They like the idea of recovery but not the work it takes to get there. They are not ready to take the road less traveled.

The road less traveled has always been the better route. Jesus said, "Enter through the narrow gate" (Matt. 7:13).

Recovery Step: Are you willing to take the road less traveled? If you are, don't wait another day to start the journey.

God's Voice

JULY 29

Years ago on Christmas Eve, a man living in a posh California neighborhood set out with his wife and children to sing Christmas carols in a poor neighborhood. When they approached their first door and began singing, a woman came out, complaining about the "noise." At several more stops, they got the same reaction. So the family went on down the road until they found a welcoming home.

The name of one of the scorned carolers was Bing Crosby. I'm sure that if any of the neighbors had recognized his voice, they would have been thrilled to have him on their porch.

That Bing Crosby's voice could go unrecognized is a travesty. But here's something worse.

Jesus said, "My sheep listen to my voice; I know them, and they follow me" (John 10:27).

Successful recovery is spiritual recovery. And that requires recognizing God's voice. Here's the key. The best way to get to know God's voice is to get to know God.

The neighbors did not recognize Bing Crosby's voice because they did not have a personal relationship with him. The same is true with God. Until you know him personally, you will not recognize his voice. As for recovery, you'll be on your own.

> **Recovery Step:** You need to know God's voice. But first, you need to know God.

Happy Endings

JULY 30

I love the story of the little boy whose mother took him to the animal shelter to pick out a dog. He chose the homeliest looking puppy but one whose tail was wagging briskly. His mom asked the boy why he picked that particular dog. The boy said, "I wanted the dog with a happy ending."

We all like happy endings. Here's the good news. We win. For those whose faith is in their Higher Power, there is coming a day when "He will wipe every tear from their eyes. There will be no more death or mourning or crying or pain" (Rev. 21:4).

You may be in a battle today—for custody of your eyes, purity of thought, and sobriety. And while you may not win every battle, you will win the war. Your story has a happy ending.

Keep your eye on the prize. There is coming a day when you will be victorious. The road ahead will be marred by potholes, occasional detours, and moments of discouragement. But I've read the end of the Book. There is a happy ending.

Recovery Step: Take a moment today to reflect on the fact that by faith in God, your journey will end well. There will be a happy ending. For that you can be thankful.

The Ship

JULY 31

There is an intriguing verse buried deep within the pages of the Old Testament: “King Jehoshaphat built a fleet of trading ships to go to Ophir for gold, but they never set sail—they were wrecked at Ezion Geber” (1 Kings 22:48).

The ships never set sail. So sad.

That is a commentary on many lives I know. Notice the order of the words. Two things happened. First, the ships stayed in the harbor; they never set sail. Second, they were wrecked.

The travesty of your life is not that you were wrecked and therefore did not set sail (fulfill your dreams). Actually, the travesty is that in not setting sail you are wrecked.

Yes, addiction can damage your ship. But it can’t sink your ship. Only you can do that. It is what happens after your discovery that matters most. If you stay safely in the harbor, that will lead to your destruction.

Recovery Step: You can stay in the harbor, but that’s not what ships were made for. So take a chance. Chase your dreams. Don’t let your past be the god of your future.

AUGUST

Prayer does not change God,
but it changes him who prays.

—Soren Kierkegaard

Channel Surfing

AUGUST 1

"David sent someone to find out about her [Bathsheba]" (2 Sam. 11:3).

Before David got into trouble with Bathsheba, he got into trouble with himself. At a time when other kings were off to war, David chose to stay back in his man cave.

It was just another spring night, and boredom set in. The couch made no demands, and the remote fit snugly in his hand. David hit the channel button at random until an alluring flicker caught his eye. Reverse. Stop. Pause. He zoomed in to watch a tantalizing scene—an intimate candlelit spa. He could almost smell the candle wax and bath oil. Although the cool evening air caused a slight haze to rise from the water, the bather's physical attributes were unmistakable.

Long before channel surfing, King David knew about channel surfing. Bored, he became curious. Curious, he became enticed. Enticed, he became trapped. Then, within minutes, it seemed like hours. It was too late. The sin had been committed.

David got into trouble because he didn't get into anything else.

Recovery Step: We get into trouble because we aren't into anything else. When you let your mind channel surf, you're done. The rest is simply the inevitable result.

Hang On to Your Harp

AUGUST 2

Psalm 137:2 says, "There on the poplars we hung our harps."

The children of God had passed from the uttermost to the guttermost. Once proud inhabitants of the land that flowed with milk and honey, they were now enslaved in the land of Babylon. Their response was understandable: "By the rivers of Babylon we sat and wept" (Ps. 137:1).

Known for their joyful music, the Israelites were asked to play music and sing songs. They responded by hanging up their harps. The music had gone out of their souls, replaced by fear, loneliness, and discouragement.

But it doesn't have to be that way. True joy is not dependent on where we are but on how we are.

Perhaps your addiction has landed you in a place of brokenness and loss. The good news is that God is still there. Lift your head, raise your voice, and look to your God. Now is not the time to hang up your harp.

Recovery Step: Keep singing, keep walking, keep looking to God. Never hang up your harp.

Three Keys to Sobriety

AUGUST 3

There is no story in literature full of more lessons than that of the Good Samaritan. After the priest and Levite passed the fallen man, a Samaritan approached. Then he did what neither religious leader dared to do. He got his hands dirty.

"He went to him and bandaged his wounds, pouring on oil and wine. Then he put the man on his own donkey, brought him to an inn and took care of him" (Luke 10:34).

Martin Luther King, Jr. wrote in *Strength to Love*, "I imagine that the first question the priest and Levite asked was: 'If I stop to help this man, what will happen to me?' But by the very nature of his concern, the good Samaritan reversed the question: 'If I don't stop to help this man, what will happen to him?'"

Jesus is the Good Samaritan who came to save us. And in this passage we discover three keys to recovery.

- The sufferer must recognize his helplessness.
- There must be surrender.
- There must be community.

Recovery Step: If you have fallen, you need three things: helplessness, surrender, and community. Miss any of these and you will miss God.

Your Weather Forecast

AUGUST 4

I have looked up the weather forecast for your area, for the next year. Here it is: There's gotta be a little rain sometime.

Rain gets a bad knock. It is vital for life on earth. When scientists begin looking for life on other planets, they begin with a search for water.

Sure, we want sunshine. But sometimes we need rain. Ben Franklin said, "When the well is dry, we know the worth of water."

If your well is dry today, if you are struggling, if you find yourself in a storm, embrace the process.

Recovery Step: "I will send you rain in its season, and the ground will yield its crops and the trees their fruit" (Lev. 26:4). If you're in a rainy season, celebrate the fact that no cloud ever forms without God's consent.

There's Still Hope

AUGUST 5

When we were considering possible names for our ministry several years ago, we immediately landed on the word *hope.* As survivors of addiction and trauma, Beth and I came to embrace hope as the fundamental key to our future. We have come to believe that no matter the past and despite all the pain, there's still hope—always.

We are standing on solid ground.

In his article "The Power of Hope," Dr. Dale Archer wrote, "The power of hope defines the psychological victim and psychological survivor."

The Bible uses the word *hope* 244 times. Here is just one example: "I pray that the eyes of your heart may be enlightened in order that you may know the hope to which he has called you" (Eph. 1:18).

Recovery Step: Do you have setbacks, struggles, and stains? Sure you do. But you also have something stronger than all that. It's called hope. Embrace that hope now.

Daily

AUGUST 6

G. K. Chesterton said, "The Christian ideal has not been tried and found wanting. It has been found difficult; and left untried."

But following Jesus isn't just hard work. It is daily work.

Jesus said, "Whoever wants to be my disciple must deny themselves and take up their cross daily and follow me" (Luke 9:23).

Catch that word: *daily*.

If you are to enjoy the benefits of recovery, I suggest you engage the following plan:

- Daily prayer
- Daily readings
- Daily surrender
- Daily denial
- Daily choices
- Daily calls

Recovery Step: Recovery has not been tried and found wanting. It has been found difficult and left untried. So let's get after it. Engage the serious work of recovery—daily.

System Restore

AUGUST 7

When Microsoft launched Windows ME (Millennial Edition), the system restore feature caused a stir. If your computer suffered a system meltdown, you could select system restore and reset your computer to a point in the past. Problem solved. Everything you somehow messed up on your computer returned to the way it was at that earlier time.

God performed a system restore of sorts on Jehoahaz. Although the king spent many years moving away from God, the moment he "sought the Lord's favor" (2 Kings 13:4), God listened to his prayer and restored him, sending a deliverer—probably some sort of ally who joined forces with Jehoahaz—to spare this king and his people from their enemies. Throughout Scripture, as individuals turned away from God and eventually returned, God stood ready to welcome them back into a relationship with him.

Every addict needs a system restore feature. The good news is that they have one. When God looks at you, he sees beyond the failure, the relapse, and the pain. Just as he restored King Jehoahaz, he will restore you.

Recovery Step: Ask God to hit your system restore button.

Turning a Blind Eye

AUGUST 8

President Teddy Roosevelt set up a boxing ring in the White House where he would spar with anyone brave enough to get in the ring. One of his aides, Dan Tyler Moore, actually blinded the President's left eye with a right hook. Roosevelt concealed the fact that he had lost his sight in order to protect the reputation of the man who detached his retina.

Moore said, "But could you ask for any better proof of the man's sportsmanship than the fact that he never told me what I had done to him?"

Putting the needs of others ahead of his own provided a glimpse into the character of Teddy Roosevelt. This same attitude will take you a long way in your sobriety.

When we think about the needs of others and get our eyes off ourselves once in a while, life comes into focus, sobriety comes within reach, and hope rises.

Recovery Step: "Do not be conformed to the pattern of this world, but be transformed by the renewing of your mind" (Rom. 12:2).

A Speeding President

AUGUST 9

Can you name the only US President to receive a warrant for speeding while in office?

Ulysses S. Grant.

The President was spotted on the streets of Washington, DC, going too fast—on his horse. Police officer William H. West pulled him over and issued a warning. The next day, West caught him again. President Grant was riding his horse as fast as ever, this time resulting in an arrest. Grant had to put up $20 rather than go to jail. He never showed up for his trial.

"Those who live only to satisfy their own sinful nature will harvest decay and death from that sinful nature" (Gal. 6:8 NLT).

Although it was just $20, even the President of the United States had to pay for his "crime." Every decision you ever make—good or bad—will have ramifications.

Robert Louis Stevenson said, "Sooner or later we all sit down to a banquet of consequences."

Recovery Step: Embrace the upside of consequences. In the words of B. F. Skinner, "The consequences of an act affect the probability of its occurring again."

Water Slides

AUGUST 10

In the 1980s, I used to go to large water parks for fun. There was a huge water park in Dallas called Wet 'N Wild, one of the largest such parks at the time. One day as I was walking around with some friends, we saw several guys at the park who were in incredible physical condition. As I recall, on average, these guys were about 6'4" and 250 pounds. After crossing paths with them several times at the water park, my curiosity got the best of me.

I approached them and asked who they were. "We are Dallas Cowboy football players," one of them said. "We are here because Coach Landry said it would be good off-season training for us to climb the steps to the top of the water slides."

Coach Landry was Tom Landry whose face would be on the "Mount Rushmore of great football coaches in history." And I love his thinking. Landry understood that if his players were going to be in their best condition during the season, they needed to prepare before the season.

Success tomorrow is dependent on preparation today. Solomon was right: "Put your outdoor work in order and get your fields ready; after that, build your house" (Prov. 24:27).

Recovery Step: Prepare today for the recovery you want tomorrow.

John Wayne

AUGUST 11

"Never apologize, mister, it's a sign of weakness."—John Wayne, *She Wore a Yellow Ribbon*, 1949

I was raised in a John Wayne household. Grown men don't cry. We don't admit it when we are wrong. And we never apologize.

Nothing could be more opposite from the biblical model. Scripture reads, "Make every effort to live in peace with everyone and to be holy" (Heb. 12:14).

I'm not going to ask you if you have said or done anything you should apologize for. I know you have. That's part of the human condition.

A better question is whether you have apologized for the pain you have caused. That's part of the 12 Steps.

In working Step 9, you make direct amends to all you have harmed whenever possible unless to do so would injure the other person. And even then, you make indirect amends or living amends. Doing nothing is not an option.

Recovery Step: Ask God who you need to make amends to and then follow his lead.

Bankrupted by Success

AUGUST 12

William "Bud" Post won $16.2 million in the Pennsylvania lottery. He figured he was set for life. But his ex-girlfriend successfully sued him for a share of his winnings. And Bud's brother hired a hit man to kill him, hoping to inherit some of the fortune. Sadly, Bud's troubles didn't end there. Due to fulfilling repeated requests for debt relief from friends and family and making a large investment in a failed business venture, Bud found himself over $1 million in debt within a year of winning the lottery. By the time he reached retirement age, the former multimillionaire was surviving on $450 a month and food stamps.

Post is not alone. Within five years of winning the jackpot, one-third of all lottery winners declare bankruptcy. Too often we put our trust in our own wisdom.

Wise Solomon offered a better way. "Trust in the Lord with all your heart and lean not on your own understanding; in all your ways submit to him, and he will make your paths straight" (Prov. 3:5–6).

Like Bud Post, you might win the lottery. But be warned: the more you have, the less you trust. Recovery is a spiritual process, one that requires complete abandonment to your Higher Power. Remember, it was trusting in your own ideas that got you in trouble in the first place.

> **Recovery Step:** Ask God for wisdom and then live based on the insight he gives.

The Cake

AUGUST 13

We do it four times a year. We bake a chocolate cake for each of the four birthdays in our family. And while the finished product is fantastic, the individual ingredients don't taste so good—raw eggs, flour, vegetable oil. But put them together and stick it in the oven for a while, and the result is awesome.

In life, the individual ingredients don't always taste so good. But God is all about the finished product.

Everything about you goes into the final product. When you bake in your past trauma, mistakes, good and bad decisions, relationships, personality, passions, and addictions, you get who you are today—a wonderful, redeemable, child of the King.

You know the verse as well as I do: "And we know that for those who love God all things work together for good, for those who are called according to his purpose" (Rom. 8:28 ESV).

"All things" means all things. God uses it all. It all goes into the cake. It all matters. It's all good in the hands of God.

Recovery Step: Trust the great Baker to use it all—the good, the bad, and the ugly—to create a finished product.

Three Shots

AUGUST 14

Two men went hunting in the woods. The game warden told them that if they got lost they should fire three shots in rapid succession to get help. Sure enough, they got lost.

While one of the men went in search of help, the other fired three shots, but no help came. So he tried it again with the same result. After a while, his partner returned. He said, "I couldn't find anyone. We're still lost."

"What should we do?" asked the other hunter.

"I think you should fire three more shots," said his friend.

"It's too late," said the first. "I've run out of arrows."

The man had great intentions. But arrows are no substitute for the sound of a gun. And good intentions are no substitute for doing the right thing.

Jesus said, "Anyone who chooses to do the will of God will find out whether my teaching comes from God or whether I speak on my own" (John 7:17). In other words, getting it right matters more than wanting to get it right.

Recovery Step: Go to meetings, make the calls, work with your sponsor. Do the things that work. Sincerity void of action gets you nowhere.

Winter

AUGUST 15

Winter is a part of life (unless you live in Florida like me).

If your marriage is in the midst of trauma, find hope in the words of one spouse to another: "My beloved spoke and said to me, 'Arise, my darling, my beautiful one, come with me. See! The winter is past; the rains are over and gone'" (Song of Sol. 2:10–11).

Journalist and naturalist Hal Borland wrote, "No winter lasts forever; no spring skips its turn."

You may be navigating an absolute blizzard right now, but spring never skips its turn. You can't force spring; you can only wait for it. But don't let winter go to waste. I suggest you take advantage of that season. Do three things.

- Find the purpose.
- Live in the present.
- Rest in the process.

Recovery Step: Accept winter as one of the seasons of life. While you're waiting on spring, let God use this season to teach you, guide you, and bless you.

The First Call

AUGUST 16

In 1876, Alexander Graham Bell placed the first phone call. He called his assistant, Thomas Watson, who was in another room in the same house. His message: "Mr. Watson, come here. I want to see you."

The telephone has come a long way in the last 150 years. Sadly, I'm old enough to remember the party line, which was phased out in the 1970s. My first cell phone doubled as a brick. A lot has changed.

My current cell number has ten digits. Until a few decades ago, we only dialed seven numbers. And there was a time when every person's landline consisted of just four digits.

Calling one another has become more complicated than ever. But at least we no longer have to make "long distance" calls—except for one. The good news is that God has caller ID, and he still picks up every time.

Recovery Step: "The Lord is near to all who call on him, to all who call on him in truth" (Ps. 145:18). Start each day with a call to the only One who always picks up and where you'll never get a busy signal.

You're Guilty

AUGUST 17

Sin can only destroy us if we let it. John said, "If we confess our sins, he is faithful and just and will forgive us our sins and purify us from all unrighteousness" (1 John 1:9).

I love the story that unfolded in a Houston courtroom in April, 1994. Arthur Hollingsworth was on trial for the armed robbery of a Sun Mart convenience store.

Harris County prosecutor Jay Hileman asked Hollingsworth, "You're guilty, aren't you?"

Hollingsworth responded, "No."

Hileman repeated, "Mr. Hollingsworth, you're guilty, aren't you?"

Hollingsworth said it again: "No."

Hileman stayed at it. "Mr. Hollingsworth, you're guilty, aren't you?"

Hollingsworth eventually caved. "Yeah, I guess I am."

Lee Strobel wrote, "Few things accelerate the peace process as much as humbly admitting our own wrongdoing and asking forgiveness."

Recovery Step: Confess your sin to God in order to receive his forgiveness and peace.

Restitution

AUGUST 18

Dr. George Simon is a leading expert on manipulators and the author of *In Sheep's Clothing*. He cites four marks of true change: acknowledgement of a wrong, the willingness to confess it, the willingness to abandon it, and the willingness to make restitution.

Did you catch that last one—restitution?

When Zacchaeus, who turned government tax fraud into a sport, came to faith in Christ, it changed everything. Zacchaeus quickly raced through the first three steps. He acknowledged that he had been robbing people of their taxes. He confessed it openly. And he committed to never doing it again. But then came the difference-maker.

"Zacchaeus stood up and said to the Lord, 'Look, Lord! Here and now I give half of my possessions to the poor, and if I have cheated anybody out of anything, I will pay back four times the amount'" (Luke 19:8).

We know we have become sober because we have quit acting out. And we know we are in recovery because we make restitution.

Recovery Step: In your addiction, you have trampled on the hearts of those you love the most. Today, find one small way to offer restitution. Make things right—one day at a time.

The Driver

AUGUST 19

When I was a kid, our family drove great distances on vacations from Texas to California, Tennessee, and Ohio. I often slept for hours in the crowded car. How could I do that? It's simple. I knew the driver. With Dad at the wheel, I always felt safe.

I have found recovery to be the most exhilarating ride of my life. But it can become very frustrating and even scary if I forget who is in the driver's seat.

I love the simple words of Martin Luther: "Pray, and let God worry." Corrie ten Boom said, "Never be afraid to trust an unknown future to a known God."

If you are afraid of relapse, I understand. If you are worried that your addicted spouse will fall, no one can blame you. But with God behind the wheel, you can be sure of this: The journey ends well.

Recovery Step: "Trust in the Lord with all your heart, and lean not on your own understanding" (Prov. 3:5).

Mack Robinson

AUGUST 20

In recovery, you cannot afford to fail. And the good news is that with God on your side, you don't have to.

The Scripture promises, "What, then, shall we say in response to these things? If God is for us, who can be against us?" (Rom. 8:31).

History reminds us of the legendary Olympics of 1936. Among the four gold medals that Jesse Owens won, the one awarded for the 200-meter run on August 5 set a new world record that day. But there is more to the story.

The world record Owens set that day broke the "old" record set just one day earlier by a 22-year-old runner named Mack Robinson. Like Owens, Robinson was a Black American running before an audience that included Adolf Hitler. Robinson was the second-fastest man in the world, having just set the world record on August 4. Owens credited Robinson with making him better. "With Mack on my team, I knew I never had to run alone," he said.

In your race for sobriety, know this: You will never have to run alone.

Recovery Step: You are running the race of your life for sobriety and recovery. Keep running, no matter what. And know this: You will never have to run alone.

Naked People

AUGUST 21

You can impress from a distance, but you can only influence up close. But how does influence work?

For answers, we turn to the wisdom of Mark Twain: "Clothes make the man. Naked people have little or no influence on society."

I've got to think there is more to influence than wearing clothes.

Jesus agrees. He said, "Let your light shine before others that they may see your good deeds and glorify your Father in heaven" (Matt. 5:16).

Did you catch that? Influence is not about what we say but what we do. It's about living an example for others to follow. So if you want to help others stay sober, stay sober yourself. If you want to lead others into recovery, do the work of recovery yourself. If you want others to be more Christlike, be more Christlike yourself.

Recovery Step: Become the person you want others to be. Let your light shine before others.

Lions and Tigers

AUGUST 22

Recently I read that in a fight, a tiger beats a lion every time. But when it's five tigers versus five lions, the lions win. Why? Because they know how to fight together.

Scripture teaches, "I appeal to you, brothers and sisters, in the name of our Lord Jesus Christ, that all of you agree with one another in what you say and that there be no divisions among you, but that you be perfectly united in mind and thought" (1 Cor. 1:10).

All of us are stronger than any of us. You need a group, and a group needs you. The opposite of addiction is connection.

I'm not a big soccer fan, but I've heard of Abby Wambach. She is a legend in her sport, a member of the Soccer Hall of Fame. She weighs in on the power of group: "I've never scored a goal in my life without getting a pass from someone else."

Recovery Step: If you plan to win at recovery, learn to score off someone else's pass. And learn to pass on your recovery as well.

Why Five Stones?

AUGUST 23

We all know the story of David and Goliath. With a single stone, the boy took down the giant. What causes consternation among theologians thousands of years later is one small part of the story. David took five stones into battle when he would only need one.

Here's my take. David had enough faith to face the giant with a slingshot but not enough faith to do it with just one stone. God used this young man with incomplete faith anyway.

Don't wait until you have complete faith—or sobriety—to enter the battle for recovery. God isn't waiting for you to get it all together before he blesses you and brings freedom. Come as you are with what faith you have to the King of the universe.

Recovery Step: Come to God with incomplete faith. Make this verse your own this week: "Being confident of this, that he who began a good work in you will carry it on to completion until the day of Christ Jesus" (Phil. 1:6).

Wheaties

AUGUST 24

In 1937, Wheaties sponsored baseball broadcasts on ninety-five radio stations across the country. It held a nationwide contest to find its most popular announcer. The winner would receive a free trip to California. The winner was a minor league play-by-play announcer from Des Moines, Iowa. He cashed in on his trip to California where he was spotted by Warner Brothers. They were impressed with his voice and good looks, so they offered him a screen test.

The man's name was Ronald Reagan.

When asked about the key to his success, young Reagan said, "Success is about being where you're supposed to be when you're supposed to be there."

Jesus said it like this: "Whoever can be trusted with little can also be trusted with much" (Luke 16:10).

Recovery is about being faithful where you are in the moment. If you are faithful where you are today, tomorrow will bring greater challenges—and rewards. It's all about making the next right decision.

Recovery Step: Be faithful where you are right now. Do the little things right, and greater challenges and blessings will come.

Liberty or Death

AUGUST 25

On March 2, 1775, Patrick Henry spoke at St. John's Church in Richmond, Virginia. He offered this famous line: "I know not what course others may take; but as for me, give me liberty or give me death!"

We should all cherish liberty as much as Patrick Henry did. Slaves to our addictions, we have been set free by God. Now we have to choose that freedom and cherish it as much as life itself.

This would be a good mantra for each of us: "Give me sobriety or give me death!"

With sobriety comes freedom. As one who has lived on both sides—addiction and freedom—I am committed to living in freedom. You can claim the freedom Jesus came to give when he said, "So if the Son sets you free, you will be free indeed" (John 8:36).

Recovery Step: You can have liberty—from porn, sex addiction, and other strongholds. But like Patrick Henry, you must really want it.

Two-for-One Deal

AUGUST 26

Saint Augustine said, "God loves each of us as if there were only one of us." There is nothing you can ever do to invalidate that love.

But life often feels like a battlefield.

Five hundred years before the birth of Jesus, God's people were discouraged. They had lost much because of their faithfulness. But God gave them this promise: "Return to your fortress, you prisoners of hope; even now I announce that I will restore twice as much to you" (Zech. 9:12).

God gives two blessings for every trouble.

Your job is to be faithful; God's job is to take care of you. And his promise is that no matter how steep the hill or tough the battle, the blessings on the other side are worth it.

God's two-for-one blessing comes with a purpose. Warren Wiersbe said, "God doesn't bless us just to make us happy; He blesses us to make us a blessing."

Recovery Step: In the midst of the battle, remain faithful. That's all God asks. And know that the blessing from him will be twice the magnitude of the trials you face to get there.

No Greater Joy

AUGUST 27

John, the dearest friend Jesus had on earth, outlived every other disciple as he developed disciples and poured his life into them. Then we find a window into John's soul in the words of his final letter.

"I have no greater joy than to hear that my children are walking in the truth" (3 John 1:4).

That reflects the greatest joy of recovery—seeing others grow in their own relationship with Christ and on their personal journey of wholeness. I suggest there are three stages of recovery. Which stage are you in today?

- Stage 1: You are not in recovery.
- Stage 2: You are in recovery.
- Stage 3: You are helping someone else find recovery.

Recovery Step: Embrace the 12th Step. "Having had a spiritual awakening as the result of these steps, we tried to carry this message to alcoholics, and to practice these principles in all our affairs."

Keep Swimming

AUGUST 28

In 1952, Florence Chadwick attempted to swim the ocean waters between Catalina Island and the California shore, through foggy weather and choppy seas. After fifteen hours, her muscles began to cramp, and her resolve began to weaken. She begged to be taken out of the water. But her mother, riding in a boat alongside, urged her to not give up. She kept trying but grew exhausted. Aides lifted her out of the water. As they paddled a few more minutes, the mist broke, and she discovered that the shore was less than a half mile away. She said, "All I could see was the fog. I think if I could have seen the shore, I would have made it."

Friend, don't give up. The finish may be only strokes away. God may at this very moment be lifting the fog. The shore is within your reach.

We all look to a day when there will be "no more death or mourning or crying or pain" (Rev. 21:4). Until that day comes, keep swimming.

Recovery Step: Keep swimming through the fog.

Marilyn Monroe

AUGUST 29

Marilyn Monroe said, "I am good, but not an angel. I do sin, but I am not the devil. I am just a small girl in a big world trying to find someone to love."

With those words, Marilyn Monroe spoke for all of us. If you struggle with compulsive behaviors, you are still a good person, locked in a struggle for sobriety and sanity.

The man closest to Jesus admitted, "If we claim to be without sin, we deceive ourselves, and the truth is not in us" (1 John 1:8).

You may feel awkward about bringing your recurring sins before the Lord. You may be embarrassed by the number of times you have had to deal with the same issues—issues that stubbornly refuse to go away. You may imagine that God is collecting a long list of repeated offenses to be used against you. But the truth is this: If you recognize your mistakes and confess them to God, he will forgive you.

The struggle will be with you for the rest of your life—every single day. You can find victory. That's God's promise. But if you fall short, you can also find forgiveness. That's God's nature.

Recovery Step: Admit you are in the battle of your life. Don't run from the battle; engage it. And commit to personal recovery today. But if you find yourself coming up short, return to the battle. More importantly, return to God.

The Water Recedes

AUGUST 30

"The waters receded" (Gen. 8:1).

With those three words, God brought an end to the epic story of the Great Flood. From the oceans to the skies, the Creator was screaming one word around the globe: Hope.

Know this. When your boat takes on water, the water will recede. When your debt consumes you, the water will recede. When it feels like your marriage can't make it, the water will recede. And when you feel the full power of addiction, the water will recede.

The water always recedes.

In his book *The Psychology of Hope*, Charles Synder offers two keys to seeing the floodwaters recede. We need willpower (what to do) and waypower (how to do it).

Recovery Step: Life is full of trials. Anyone who tells you there will be no floods is messing with you. But you can bank on this: The waters recede.

Family Dinners

AUGUST 31

This may be the most surprising key to sobriety: family dinners.

A study by Columbia University found that the power of communication and role-modeling during family dinner is hard to overstate. The study concluded that teens whose families dine together are four times less likely to smoke, 2.5 times less likely to use marijuana, and half as likely to drink.

Author Julie Kendrick cites "misery and mayhem" as byproducts of missed family meals.

Stanford University conducted a study that concluded that frequent family dinners have significant benefits, including mental health and stability.

Sometimes we make sobriety too difficult. Simply sitting down with our family over dinner each night will provide blessings of serenity, sobriety, and so much more.

Recovery Step: The Bible commands parents to teach God's principles to their children "when you sit at home and when you walk along the road, when you lie down and when you get up" (Deut. 6:7). Start with regular family dinners.

SEPTEMBER

Jesus went out as usual to the Mount of Olives,
and his disciples followed him.
On reaching the place, he said to them,
"Pray that you will not fall into temptation."

—Luke 22:39–40

57 Rules

SEPTEMBER 1

A sign hanging on a wall in a small business read, "The 57 Rules of Success: Rule #1: Deliver the goods. Rule #2: The other 56 rules don't matter."

When I was a young boy, we had a milkman who "delivered the goods" right to our front door. The grocery store did the same thing. Mom never accepted excuses. They either delivered the goods or they were in real trouble.

Jesus "delivered the goods" like no man before or after. But he kept things pretty simple. While the religious crowd was all about rules, Jesus had just one for his earliest followers. When he saw these would-be disciples, Jesus said, "Come, follow me" (Matt. 4:19).

Sure, other rules would follow—rules about how to love God and others, rules about how to care for the hurting and minister to the poor. But it was Rule #1 that served as a foundation for all the others. "Come, follow me."

Saint Augustine said it like this: "Love God and do whatever you please."

The Christian life is not about rules; it's about relationship. And that's good news for those of us with hurts, habits, and hang-ups. Jesus didn't tell Peter, James, and John to figure it all out and then follow him. Why? Because we can't figure it all out until we follow him.

Recovery Step: Follow Jesus today. Save the rest of the rules for later.

The Last Ten Feet

SEPTEMBER 2

Can you ever quit doing recovery work? What if you have ten years of sobriety? Or twenty?

I love the way Dr. Milton Magness says it: "You might outgrow addiction, but you'll never outgrow recovery."

Let me use an analogy. Imagine that you are climbing a 14,000-foot mountain. The more you climb and the higher you go, the better you become at mountain climbing. But (and this is a big "but") you must work just as hard on the last ten feet of the climb as you did on the first ten feet of the climb.

Starting the journey is critical, but finishing is epic. God is all about strong finishes. The Bible reminds us, "He who began a good work in you will complete it" (Phil. 1:6).

To you who are new to recovery, welcome to the journey! To you who have been at this for a while, press on. Keep going. Never stop. The rest of your journey will be the best of your journey.

Recovery Step: Keep climbing.

Chase the Kangaroo

SEPTEMBER 3

In *Chase the Kangaroo*, Charles Cos wrote, "God calls me to be faithful. The end result is in his hands, not mine."

That flies in the face of our results-driven world. We live in an age whose god is the scoreboard, bank balance, and bathroom scale. The ends don't merely justify the means; the means no longer matter.

But in God's playbook, the game is the scoreboard. How you play the game matters. Then, when the game is over, the scoreboard goes black and the players are carried off the field on the backs of angels.

In recovery, pay close attention to the journey. The destination will take care of itself.

Samuel said, "Be sure to fear the Lord and serve him faithfully with all your heart; consider what great things he has done for you" (1 Sam. 12:24).

Today, don't choose to be great, successful, or happy. Choose to be faithful.

Recovery Step: Walk faithfully before the Lord today. Then leave the rest in his enormous hands.

Take a Bow

SEPTEMBER 4

Martin Luther had a professor who did the same thing every time he walked into the classroom. After he hung up his coat, he walked over to each student and bowed. One day, Luther got up the courage to ask him why he bowed before each student.

The professor explained, "I bow before you in honor of what you might become if you get your life in tune with God."

We all have a choice. We can focus on what we have been or on what we might become. God chooses the latter.

Paul wrote, "Now to him who is able to do immeasurably more than all we ask or imagine, according to his power that is at work within us" (Eph. 3:20).

I wish I could be with you in person today. If I could, I'd say, "Great job! While 90 percent of sex addicts never get any help for their disease, you are reading this daily devotion written by a fellow addict, hoping that this might be the day he finally says something really good!"

I honor you for joining me on this road to recovery. More importantly, God honors you, not because of what you've been but for what you will become.

Recovery Step: Think about all you can become. Then take a bow.

Unprocessed Shame

SEPTEMBER 5

Debbie Ford has written a helpful book, *Why Good People Do Bad Things*. She writes of the battle of good versus evil that is common to each of us, the war between good and bad, light and dark.

Then Ford offers great insight on the real problem that holds so many of us back. She says that the real obstacle to recovery is not the bad that we have done, but what she calls "unprocessed shame."

One night, Peter promised Jesus he would never deny him. And then he denied him—three times. A short time later, Jesus asked Peter, "Do you love me?" (John 21:17). When Peter admitted he loved Jesus but not with the highest form of love—*agape* love—Jesus didn't blink. He said, essentially, "That's okay. I'll use you anyway."

You have made mistakes—serious mistakes. And you've paid the price. So now it's time to move on. It's time to process your shame.

Recovery Step: Think about the thing you've done that has brought you the most shame. Then turn it over to God—and move on.

The Dumpster

SEPTEMBER 6

Imagine that you saw a man hanging around a dumpster. He looked hungry, so you gave him a $100 gift card to the supermarket just a few steps away. With that card he could purchase anything he wanted—steak, seafood, snacks, desserts, or produce. Your gift card would supply him with enough meals to last several days.

The man took your gift card with a smile and thanked you for your kindness. Then you drove away.

A couple hours later, your errands returned you to that same parking lot. And to your dismay, you found your new friend digging for food in the dumpster.

To live in our addiction is like eating out of a dumpster with a supermarket next door.

God has put recovery, fulfillment, and transformation within your reach. You can claim the freedom he offers or you can continue to eat out of the dumpster.

The Bible says, "Sovereign Lord, you are God! Your covenant is trustworthy, and you have promised these good things to your servant" (2 Sam. 7:28).

Recovery Step: A. W. Tozer said, "The goodness of God is infinitely more wonderful than we will ever be able to comprehend." You have a choice. You can walk in that goodness today, or you can return to the dumpster that never satisfies.

Banquet of Consequences

SEPTEMBER 7

We hear it all the time. "Life isn't fair." But is that really true?

It's not fair that you were emotionally abandoned by your parents. Abuse isn't fair. Neglect, family history, maltreatment—none of them are fair.

The American Psychiatric Association states that three million children experience abuse in America each year. The World Health Organization says that abuse comes in four forms: physical, sexual, emotional, and psychological. It's all abuse, and none of it is fair.

But at some point we are responsible for our own decisions. What happens to us is not our fault, but our destructive responses are.

The prophet Obadiah said, "The day of the Lord is near for all nations. As you have done, it will be done to you; your deeds will return upon your own head" (Obad. 15).

Robert Louis Stevenson said it like this: "Sooner or later we all sit down to a banquet of consequences."

Your choices bring a banquet of consequences. You can blame your past or you can change your future. Those are your two options.

Recovery Step: Which way will you go? You can blame your past or you can change your future. The next step is yours.

How Does God Deliver?

SEPTEMBER 8

Is recovery an event or a process?

In other words, when God delivers us from sexual addiction, does it happen all at once, perhaps as the result of heartfelt repentance, prayer, or inner healing? Or does deliverance come over a period of time?

In my experience and observation, while God can deliver us instantaneously, he rarely does. In fact, I'm glad—at least in my case—that deliverance has been a process. I have come to believe that the goal of recovery actually is the process itself. It is the daily work, spiritual disciplines, and daily connection that not only provide deliverance but are deliverance.

God has planned your deliverance. Never try to short-circuit God's plans.

Recovery Step: We have this promise from God: "The righteous cry out, and the Lord hears them; he delivers them from all their troubles" (Ps. 34:17). Here's the right response. Let God deliver you—on his terms.

Falling Forward

SEPTEMBER 9

Chuck Swindoll wrote a book decades ago called *Three Steps Forward, Two Steps Back* in 1998. His premise was that we all fail. And we all fall. What matters most, he wrote, was not whether we fall, but how we fall. The fall is only a permanent failure if we don't learn from it. By letting God use the mistakes of our past, we learn to fall forward.

John wrote, "Everyone born of God overcomes the world. This is the victory that has overcome the world, even our faith" (1 John 5:4).

Soichiro Honda understood a little bit about failure. He built bicycles for a living, with a focus on small motors he would attach to the bikes. Have you ever heard of the Honda Bike Company? Probably not. But you may have heard of the Honda Motor Company. When the bike thing didn't work out, Honda put all his efforts into making cars. What he began in a simple shop in 1948 evolved into one of the premier companies in the world. The key? Soichiro Honda fell forward. Looking back at the keys to his success, he wrote, "Success is 99 percent failure."

Just remember—when you fall, fall forward.

Recovery Step: In what ways have you failed? Bring your past before God. Then turn the page to a whole new beginning.

Know when to Run

SEPTEMBER 10

You have to know when to run. You have to know when to walk away. You have to know when to wait.

That is the story of every addict. And never was there a harder lesson for me to learn. In my addict mind, I could always hang around the fantasy and lust. I could walk up to the line, able to back away at the last second. It took decades for me to learn to not only walk away but to run!

You have gambled with your habit for long enough. It's time to fold 'em. It's time to walk away. It's time to run.

> **Recovery Step:** Jesus said, "For whoever wants to save their life will lose it, but whoever loses their life for me will find it" (Matt. 16:25). We need to walk away from our own ways and run to Jesus.

Life Change

SEPTEMBER 11

Rarely does life change occur void of brokenness.

Only those who have learned well to be dissatisfied with themselves become truly satisfied with Christ.

Rarely does life change occur void of brokenness.

When God's children refused to bow to him, he pronounced a plague of locusts. But being the God that he is, he also said that if they repented of their ways and committed to true life change, there was hope beyond what they deserved. God said, "'Even now,' declares the Lord, 'return to me with all your heart, with fasting and weeping and mourning'" (Joel 2:12).

Rarely does life change occur void of brokenness.

Recovery Step: Let the damage of your addiction sink in. Take a moment to consider the cost it has brought to your life and to others. Let the pain of your actions bring a brokenness to your heart. Why? Because rarely does life change occur void of brokenness.

Why Me?

SEPTEMBER 12

Arthur Ashe, the legendary Wimbledon tennis champion, was dying of AIDS, which he contracted when he received infected blood during heart surgery in 1983. During his illness, Ashe received thousands of encouraging letters. In one letter, the fan asked, "Why did God have to select you for such a horrible disease?"

Ashe wrote back:

> The world over—50 million children start playing tennis; 5 million learn to play tennis; 500,000 learn professional tennis; 50,000 come to the circuit; 5,000 reach the grand slam; 50 reach Wimbledon; 4 to semi-finals; 2 to the finals; when I was holding a cup, I never asked God, "Why me?" And today in pain I should be asking God "Why me?"

I suggest that rather than focusing on the injustices that went against you, focus on the injustices that went in your favor. The Bible promises, "God treats us much better than we deserve" (Rom. 3:24 CEV).

Recovery Step: When you go through hard times, remind yourself that they only seem "hard" because you've had so many good times. Count your blessings. Name them one by one.

Universal Principle

SEPTEMBER 13

There is a universal principle that applies to addiction. It's called sowing and reaping. The ancient prophet Hosea said, "Plant the good seeds of righteousness, and you will harvest a crop of love" (Hos. 10:12 NLT).

The mistake most of us make is that we want good results without doing the things that produce those results. We want the blessing of the crop without the pain of the work.

Muhammad Ali said, "The fight is won or lost far away from witnesses, behind the lines, in the gym, and out there on the road long before I dance under those lights."

Recovery is never won in the first round. You have to go the distance. But tomorrow's victory is decided by today's work. If you want to be well tomorrow, you need to pray today. If you want to be strong tomorrow, go to a meeting tonight. If you want to see a good harvest, start planting seeds now.

Everything significant that happens to you tomorrow will have already been determined by the things you did today. What you sow today you will reap tomorrow. That is a universal principle of life.

Recovery Step: Do one thing today that will fuel your recovery tomorrow.

Climbing Blind

SEPTEMBER 14

On May 25, 2001, Erik Weihenmayer reached the summit of Mount Everest. A year later, he completed the Seven Summits, climbing the highest peak on each of the seven continents. By doing so, he accomplished what only 150 others have ever done. But with Weihenmayer, there was one difference.

Erik Weihenmayer is completely blind.

But he wasn't done yet. Erik went on to kayak 277 miles down the treacherous Colorado River.

That is the definition of faith: "Confidence in what we hope for and assurance about what we do not see" (Heb. 11:1).

Sometimes in recovery it feels like we are flying blind. You will be called upon to do things you never saw coming when you started this journey—things like a personal inventory, a therapeutic disclosure, amends, and sponsoring others.

My suggestion is that you do what Erik Weihenmayer did. Even when you can't see the way ahead, keep climbing. Never quit.

Recovery Step: Move forward by faith.

Don't Ever Do This!

SEPTEMBER 15

In about 760 BC, the prophet Amos in Judah said something that every recovering addict needs to hear: "Woe to you who are complacent" (Amos 6:1).

Never ever take your sobriety for granted. Never ever, ever, ever. Don't do it. Never.

There will be days when you think you've "got this" and that you can take your foot off the pedal and coast for a while. Don't do it! Never become complacent.

So how do you overcome complacency? Kerry Siggins, host of the *Leadership* podcast, offers five great suggestions.

- Ask for feedback.
- Take on a new endeavor.
- Anticipate change.
- Read more.
- Don't drink your own Kool-Aid.

Your past performance is no guarantee of future success. Keep moving forward. Never look back. And don't ever become complacent. Ever.

Recovery Step: Pray for a spirit of determination and consistency.

Five Grains of Gratitude

SEPTEMBER 16

When the Pilgrims landed at Plymouth Rock in 1620, they faced harsh conditions. When they became desperate for food, Governor William Bradford rationed five grains of corn per day for each person. When things got better, Bradford did not want the people to forget what they had gone through, so at every Thanksgiving meal, he had five grains of corn placed at each plate.

The value of gratitude cannot be overstated; it is the great reminder of God's goodness.

We all need grains of gratitude, reminders that God's providence from yesterday points toward his sufficiency for tomorrow.

Paul said it quite simply: "In everything give thanks" (1 Thess. 5:18 KJV). Notice that he didn't say to thank God for everything, but in everything.

Recovery Step: You have two options. You can complain about your problems or you can celebrate your blessings. Only one of those will help you find recovery.

The Ultimate Sign of Recovery

SEPTEMBER 17

The year was 1919. A young man recovering from World War I injuries rented a small apartment in Chicago. He chose the location so he could be close to an author named Sherwood Anderson. He was an aspiring writer himself, so he spent as much time with Anderson as he could. For months, they talked every day. Anderson taught his mentee everything he knew about writing. The name of the young man was Ernest Hemmingway.

John Maxwell said, "A leader who produces other leaders multiplies their influences."

And that is the sign of true recovery. Ultimately, your recovery is not about you but about those you will help. Nothing brings me more joy in my own recovery than to see a man I have sponsored become a sponsor to someone else.

There once lived a famous evangelist named Elijah. He did some pretty remarkable things in his career. But the time had come for a new man to replace him—a fellow named Elisha. Elisha wanted the blessing, power, and experience of his mentor. That hope was fulfilled. "The company of the prophets from Jericho, who were watching, said, 'The spirit of Elijah is resting on Elisha'" (2 Kings 2:15).

Recovery Step: Who helped you find recovery? Who are you helping now?

Sliding Socks

SEPTEMBER 18

There's only one person who doesn't have any hidden struggles. That is the person you haven't met. Once you get to know them, you will discover they are just like everyone else. They have personal struggles that are not always obvious to the rest of us.

Someone said, "I walk around like everything's fine, but deep down, inside my shoe, my sock is sliding off."

If your sock is sliding off, you need to tell someone. Otherwise, that "sock" will drive you crazy. Eventually, it will affect your walk in irreparable ways.

The Bible advises, "Therefore confess your sins to each other and pray for each other so that you may be healed. The prayer of a righteous person is powerful and effective" (James 5:16). The Greek word for *confess* is *ekzomologeo*, which means to declare, to speak out loud, to divulge or blurt.

If you want true healing, tell someone about the sock that keeps sliding off.

Recovery Step: If you are harboring a personal fault or struggle in secret, bring it to the light with someone you can trust.

What God Requires

SEPTEMBER 19

There are a lot of character traits that you should strive for. But God got specific with a few that rise above the rest. The prophet Micah declared, "And what does the Lord require of you? To act justly and to love mercy and to walk humbly with your God" (Mic. 6:8).

Let's focus on that last one: to walk humbly with your God.

Saint Augustine said, "It was pride that changed angels into devils; it is humility that makes men as angels."

Humility is the gift that keeps on giving. The benefits of staying humble are endless. Dr. Anna Schaffner, professor at the University of Kent, identifies just a few of those benefits:

- Less stress
- Fewer negative experiences with others
- Better physical health
- Increased positive emotions
- Self-forgiveness

Humility isn't a condition; it is a choice that must be made every day. So for today, choose humility. Then, when you get up tomorrow, do it again.

Recovery Step: Walk humbly with your God.

Make God a Debtor

SEPTEMBER 20

As a pastor, I preached from a verse in Malachi many times when I was trying to drive home the command of tithing.

"'Bring the whole tithe into the storehouse, that there may be food in my house. Test me in this,' says the Lord Almighty, 'and see if I will not throw open the floodgates of heaven and pour out so much blessing that there will not be room enough to store it'" (Mal. 3:10).

As much as this passage speaks to financial giving, it is really analogous to life on every level. Take recovery, for example.

The more you give of yourself to God, the more you open your life to be blessed—with sobriety, peace of mind, authentic relationships, and serenity.

Charles Stanley was right: "You can't make a debtor out of God. You will never match what he will do for you. It's just that simple."

Recovery Step: Give to God. Give him your time, your talents, and your treasure. Try to make God a debtor, and it can't be done. But it's fun to try.

A Predictable Path

SEPTEMBER 21

"Amaziah was twenty-five years old when he became king, and he reigned in Jerusalem twenty-nine years. . . . He did what was right in the eyes of the Lord, but not wholeheartedly" (2 Chron. 25:1–2).

Amaziah became king at an age when most of us are still trying to graduate from college. To his credit, the Bible says "he did right in the eyes of the Lord." King Amaziah made a habit of doing the right thing. But then we read the rest of the story: "but not wholeheartedly."

That is many of us. We go through the motions. We attend meetings, do Step work, make calls, and check the boxes. But we are not all in. Eventually, what happened to Amaziah happens to us.

Amaziah defeated the Edomite army. That was good. But then he dabbled in false gods, bringing home a few trinkets as spoils. These trinkets became idols. And before long, the king's halfhearted ways doomed him and his people to a period of loss and failure.

Doing the right thing is wonderful. Doing it wholeheartedly is epic.

Recovery Step: Do the work of recovery wholeheartedly.

Cleaning House

SEPTEMBER 22

We used to have a cocker spaniel named Duffy. She was one happy mess. Her bladder was unable to control her joy. We were always cleaning up after her. She slobbered horribly. When she ran or shook her head, slobber went everywhere. What she messed up, we cleaned up.

One day, due to a back problem that is common among cocker spaniels, Duffy became paralyzed. She couldn't walk or get to her food dish. We spent a king's ransom on her back surgery, knowing it may not be successful. Then we had to just wait and see. We fed her by hand and carried her outside where she could at least enjoy the view.

It took a few weeks, but eventually she began to move again, and she fully recovered. But she was still a mess. So why did we continue to clean up after her, no matter how bad it got? It's simple. We loved our dog more than we hated her mess.

You are a mess. But know this. God loves you more than he hates your mess.

We have this guarantee from God: "Their sins and lawless acts I will remember no more" (Heb. 10:17). That's a pretty amazing promise.

Recovery Step: Live like a child of the King. And if you ever make a mess of things again, remember this: God loves you more than he hates your mess.

Attitude Shift

SEPTEMBER 23

Cognitive neuroscientist Dr. Caroline Leaf specializes in brain neuroplasticity. She writes, "What you are thinking every moment of every day becomes a physical reality in your brain and body, which affects your optimal mental and physical health. These thoughts collectively form your attitude, which is your state of mind, and it's your attitude and not your DNA that determines much of the quality of your life."

Did you get that? It's your attitude that determines the quality of your life.

Let me say it another way. Life is 10 percent what happens to you and 90 percent how you respond. I have found that whether I expect to have a good day or a bad day, my expectations will be met.

Now, think recovery. If your attitude is that you are a victim, hopelessly mired in your addiction, you will live in that pit. But if your attitude is that you are an overcomer, you will overcome.

Recovery Step: Pray the prayer that David prayed: "Test me and know my anxious thoughts" (Ps. 139:23).

Rule #101

SEPTEMBER 24

A few years ago, I wrote my tenth recovery book, *Recovery Rules*. It contains 100 truisms. They are pithy, easy-to-remember statements about recovery. If I could add a 101st rule, this would be it: What you tolerate today will dominate tomorrow.

If I tolerate staring at attractive women, those fantasies will dominate my mind tomorrow. If I tolerate missed recovery meetings, that absence will dominate me tomorrow. If I tolerate my middle circle behaviors today, they will dominate me tomorrow.

If Paul had written a book of recovery truisms, I'm pretty sure he would have included this: "Do not give the devil a foothold" (Eph. 4:27).

Are you going to welcome the devil into your home and give him a seat at the head of the table? Of course not! And he isn't asking for that. He just wants you to crack open the door when he comes knocking.

And then it's over.

Recovery Step: Be careful about what you tolerate.

Fun for a Season

SEPTEMBER 25

A crazy thing happened one day on the streets of Wilkes-Barre, Pennsylvania. A man was walking down the street when he found a wallet. When he opened it, he discovered hundreds of dollars in cash, as well as a driver's license. The wallet belonged to a man who was performing in town that week: Steve Martin. Now he had a choice: keep the cash or return the wallet. He returned the wallet, refusing a generous reward. He could have enjoyed the cash—for a time.

Sin is fun—for a season. That is why we need to adopt Moses's attitude. The Bible says, "He chose to be mistreated along with the people of God rather than to enjoy the pleasures of sin" (Heb. 11:25).

Acting out our addictions brings instant gratification. But I've never met a man or woman who looked back at those periods in their lives and said, "Feeding the pleasure of my addiction was a good idea." God has a better plan. Trade the pleasures of the moment for blessings that will never end.

Recovery Step: Identify one bad habit or addiction in your life. Recognize the pleasure it may bring in the moment. Then confess it to God and trade up for his blessings that have no end.

The Spite House

SEPTEMBER 26

The year was 1882. The city was New York. Real estate developer Hyman Sarner planned the erection of a new four-story apartment building. Standing in his way was a tiny strip of land owned by eccentric millionaire Joseph Richardson. That parcel of land was 5 feet wide and 104 feet long.

Sarner offered Richardson $1,000 for the land. Richardson turned him down, demanding $5,000, an astounding figure for that era. After first refusing, Sarner eventually accepted Richardson's request. But out of spite, Richardson turned him down. Worse still, he built his own structure, a 5-foot wide, four-story home, tall enough to obstruct the window views from Sarner's new apartments. Then he moved in and lived there until his death fifteen years later.

Because Richardson built the house out of spite, his home became known as the "Spite House."

"Get rid of all bitterness" (Eph. 4:31).

Recovery Step: Few things drive addiction more than resentment. When bad things happen, you have two responses at your disposal. Like Joseph Richardson, you can become bitter. Or you can get better.

I Write the Songs

SEPTEMBER 27

Okay, fellow Barry Manilow fans, get ready to be disappointed. You are familiar with his most popular song, "I Write the Songs." Here's the sad part. Barry Manilow didn't write that song.

"I Write the Songs" was actually written by Bruce Johnston of the Beach Boys. The 1976 hit won the Grammy Award for Song of the Year, but Manilow didn't write it.

Manilow was actually reluctant to record the song, stating, "The problem with the song was that if you didn't listen carefully to the lyric, you would think that the singer was singing about himself. It could be interpreted as a monumental ego trip."

That's a danger we all face—taking credit for something we did not achieve on our own. Take recovery, for example. Every time I receive another chip marking another year of sobriety, I wish I could break the chip into small pieces and give part of it to my sponsor, my past sponsors, my wife, my therapist, and each of you.

Recovery Step: Paul said, "They urgently pleaded with us for the privilege of sharing in this service to the Lord's people" (2 Cor. 8:4). No one writes the songs without a whole lot of help.

Minimizing

SEPTEMBER 28

In the 1975 movie *Monty Python and the Holy Grail*, the Black Knight (John Clease) lost both arms in the heat of combat. He said to King Arthur (Graham Chapman), "It's just a flesh wound."

The Black Knight did what addicts of all stripes have been doing since the Garden of Eden. He minimized.

We only find freedom when we obey God's command: "If we confess our sins, he is faithful and just and will forgive us our sins and purify us from all unrighteousness" (1 John 1:9).

Note the key word: *if*—"If we confess our sins."

You will never get ahead in your recovery by minimizing what you have done. Don't let your past control you. But you do need to let it inform you.

Recovery Step: Don't minimize the damage of your past. Face up to it, turn from it, and then move on.

Ten Questions

SEPTEMBER 29

King David prayed, “Search me, God, and know my heart; test me and know my anxious thoughts” (Ps. 139:23–24).

Self-reflection is a huge part of the recovery process. To that end, let me suggest ten questions to ask yourself on a daily basis. At least, ask them at the end of today.

1. Did I read Scripture today?
2. Did I read any recovery material today?
3. Am I holding onto any resentments?
4. Am I helping anyone else with their recovery?
5. Have I been 100 percent honest today?
6. Have I maintained custody of my eyes today?
7. Have I been on social media too much today?
8. Do I have firm guardrails in place?
9. Am I keeping any secrets?
10. Have I had a Recovery Day in the last month?

Recovery Step: Hang onto this list. Ask yourself these questions at the end of each day.

Your Stash

SEPTEMBER 30

I read about a bank robbery that resulted in a two-week trial for the prime suspect. While most observers were convinced of the man's guilt, the jury foreman announced the verdict: "Not guilty."

The judge then asked the defendant if he had any questions. The man replied, "Only one question, your honor. Does this mean I can keep the money?"

One way or another, the truth always comes out. The Bible warns, "You may be sure that your sin will find you out" (Num. 32:23).

The bank robber had stashed the cash. Here's my question: What have you stashed? What is it that you are holding onto today? I suggest you bring it into the light. If you don't, God will.

Recovery Step: Trash your stash.

OCTOBER

Sacrifice, discipline, and prayer are essential. We gain strength through God's Word. . . . And when we fumble due to sin—and it's gonna happen—confession puts us back on the field.

—Lou Holtz

Detours

OCTOBER 1

Those who live in the North know just two seasons: winter and road repair. The harsh winter conditions bring ice and snow, which often buckle roads and create potholes. The result is that drivers in March and April are often faced with detours from their normal routes.

Some detours are the fault of the driver—a missed turn, lack of concentration, or refusal to ask for directions. They all mean rerouting our course. So we take detours.

Barbara Bush said, "When you come to a roadblock, take a detour."

Zig Ziglar added, "Failure is a detour, not a dead end street."

For many of us, our detour led us into a life of addiction. When we should have turned right, we went left. When we should have been in the Word, we were in the world.

Jesus said, "I am the way" (John 14:6). Your habit has taken you off course. But it doesn't have to be a dead end. Follow Jesus back onto the road of sobriety and real recovery.

Recovery Step: If you have drifted off course, it's not too late to get back on the main road. Follow Jesus. He is the only One who can take you where you want to be.

The Sun Will Rise Again

OCTOBER 2

When the sun sets on Barrow, Alaska, in mid-November, it won't be seen again until late January. But no one doubts the sun's existence just because they don't see it for a while. Why? They know the sun is still there because they've seen it before.

You can be certain of God's presence because you've seen it before.

The prophet Isaiah proclaimed his confidence in a steady God. "Surely God is my salvation; I will trust and not be afraid. The Lord, the Lord himself, is my strength and my defense; he has become my salvation" (Isa. 12:2).

Isaiah had seen God before (Isa. 6); he knew he'd see him again.

The sun is doing its work just as much when it is dark outside as when it is light. God is busy, doing for us what we cannot do for ourselves, when we see him and when we don't. You can trust him today because he has been faithful all along.

Recovery Step: Trust the process. Trust the program. Trust the Savior. Chuck Swindoll said, "As followers of our Lord we believe he leads us in a certain direction in pursuit of a precise goal."

Steve Martin on Church

OCTOBER 3

"Let us consider how we may spur one another on toward good deeds, not giving up meeting together, as some are in the habit of doing" (Heb. 10:24–25).

When it comes to church attendance, a lot of us are like comedian Steve Martin who said, "I believe in going to church every Sunday, unless there's a game on."

If you are in recovery, let me make the case for going to church. The biblical command should be enough for you, but if it's not, consider these practical benefits of church for recovery.

- Connection: with your Higher Power
- Community: with others who can help you
- Correction: from the Word of God

Recovery Step: I have known hundreds of men and women who said that when they sought the will of God, he told them to get into church. I have yet to meet a person who said that God told them to leave the church. Get back into church. Do it for yourself, your family, and your recovery.

Never Satisfied

OCTOBER 4

Lust is progressive. It never satisfies. There's an old story about God's people returning from exile to Jerusalem. They started to rebuild the Temple, but when they faced opposition, they quit. In frustration, they turned inward, building lavish homes for themselves instead of furnishing God's house. For them, life was about taking the easy path and indulging in the pleasure of the moment.

Then in stepped a prophet named Haggai. He wrote, "Look at what's happening to you! You have planted much but harvest little. You eat but are not satisfied. You drink but are still thirsty" (Hag. 1:5–6 NLT).

That is the picture of every addict. We eat but are still hungry. We drink but are still thirsty. There's a reason for this.

We are chasing temporary solutions to permanent problems. Every day we are tempted to drink in the lust. And it feels good in the moment. But it only coats the real pain. What's the solution? Drink of the Living Water that never runs dry.

Recovery Step: Turn to Jesus today. Bring him your hurts, habits, and hang-ups. Then leave them there.

Truth

OCTOBER 5

In an old episode of *Bonanza*, Ben Cartwright said, "I don't have anything against education—as long as it doesn't interfere with your thinking."

That's how a lot of us think. We are all in for truth—as long as it fits our narrative.

I agree with the sage philosopher of the past generation, Elvis Presley, who said, "Truth is like the sun. You can shut it out for a time, but it ain't goin' away."

I suspect the reason we aren't always real quick to seek the truth is because the truth can be really uncomfortable. As President James Garfield said, "The truth will set you free, but first it will make you miserable."

If you are to walk in freedom, you must embrace the truth that will set you free.

Recovery Step: Jesus said that if you seek truth, you will find it (Matt. 7:7). But be warned. Before you can deal with the truth, you must let it deal with you.

Win the Morning

OCTOBER 6

Admiral William McRaven wrote a bestselling book called *Make Your Bed* where he identified numerous implications of one positive action taken each morning.

Success coach Tim Ferriss said, "If you win the morning, you win the day."

And the psalmist prayed, "Let the morning bring me word of your unfailing love" (Ps. 143:8).

Morning is everything. I suggest a morning routine that consists of the following:

- Spend five minutes in the Word.
- Spend five minutes in prayer.
- Spend five minutes reading recovery material.

Will any of this guarantee a successful day? No. But failure to capture the morning will pretty much guarantee failure throughout the day. You need to put a win on the board as early as you can each day. Don't find yourself down by ten points at the end of the first quarter.

Recovery Step: Make mornings count.

Call for Backup

OCTOBER 7

A young man decided to join the police force. As a recruit, he was asked during the exam, "What would you do if you had to arrest your own mother?"

He answered, "Call for backup."

We all need to call for backup from time to time. We weren't created to do life, let alone recovery, on our own. A lone sheep is a dead sheep. The opposite of addiction is connection.

You get the point.

Paul said, "Carry each other's burdens" (Gal. 6:2). Why did Paul say that? Maybe it was because even he, the great leader of the Christian movement, needed the support of others. That's why he had Barnabas. And Silas. And Timothy. And Luke. And John Mark. And many more.

There are days in your recovery when you don't really need anyone else in order to stay sober. But there are more days when you do. That's why you need to always have someone ready for backup.

Recovery Step: Identify someone you can call for backup.

Amber Alerts

OCTOBER 8

We are all familiar with Amber alerts in America. They are alerts that go out over everyone's smartphones to notify us that someone has suddenly gone missing. But where did Amber alerts begin?

The girl behind the Amber alerts was Amber Hagerman, a nine-year-old Girl Scout from Arlington, Texas. She was kidnapped while riding her bike on January 13, 1996. Despite a massive search, Amber was never seen alive again. Her body was found five days later about four miles from the site of her abduction. Her killer was never found.

As horrific as the loss of this precious little girl was, it sparked something positive. Because of Amber's loss and the response of those closest to her, untold numbers of others have been saved.

God takes what is destructive and indescribably painful and makes something good out of it. That doesn't erase the pain of the loss, but it does make for a better future.

The Bible says, "Come and see what God has done, his awesome deeds for mankind!" (Ps. 66:5).

Recovery Step: Lean into God today, and he will make something wonderful from the lowest points of your past.

Conquering Mountains

OCTOBER 9

Edmund Hillary, the first man to scale Mount Everest in 1953, said, "It's not the mountain we conquer, but ourselves."

The greatest mountain you may ever climb is Mount Recovery. And Hillary is right. The challenge is not the mountain; the challenge is you.

One day, Jesus climbed a mountain. "Jesus took with him Peter, James, and John the brother of James, and led them up a high mountain by themselves" (Matt. 17:1).

From this simple verse we learn quite a bit about climbing mountains. We learn that we cannot do it alone. We've all heard of Edmund Hillary. But you may have never heard of Tenzing Norgay, Hillary's climbing partner. Even Jesus didn't climb the mountain by himself. If you are to scale Mount Recovery, you'll need others along the journey.

Jesus didn't say, "There it is, boys, get after it!" He led them. In recovery, we need the help of experienced climbers. You need a mentor, someone who knows the way to the top.

Recovery Step: Mount Recovery is right in front of you. It's a tall climb, but with the right Guide and support, it can be the most important climb of your life. It's time to get started.

Seinfeld

OCTOBER 10

In a popular *Seinfeld* scene, there is this poignant interchange between Jerry and Elaine:

Jerry: "Is this about me?"
Elaine: "No."
Jerry: "Then I've lost interest."

That is the problem for most of us. If something is not about us, we aren't interested. But recovery takes us down a different path—one that values others and sacrifices our own self-interests for the sake of those we say we love.

Today, chart a different path. Put someone else's needs ahead of your own.

The addict calls that working the 12th Step. The Bible calls it sacrifice, obedience, and surrender. I call it doing the next right thing.

Recovery Step: "Do nothing out of selfish ambition or vain conceit. Rather, in humility value others above yourselves" (Phil. 2:3).

Snatched from the Fire

OCTOBER 11

Speaking of substance abuse, Joanne Zuhl wrote, "Even if addiction isn't what puts people on the streets, it's often what keeps them there."

Let's apply that to any addiction, including sex. For many of us, regardless of how we found our way into the ditch, we are there, and we struggle mightily to dig our way out. In fact, we were really destined to lives of hopelessness.

That's when the words of the prophet Zechariah bring hope, when he spoke of being "snatched from the fire" (Zech. 3:2).

Some ditches are simply too deep. You can't dig out of them. But praise God for the reach of his arm. He stands ready to snatch you from the fire.

Recovery Step: When you come to the end of yourself, you come to the beginning of God. Want to be snatched from the fire? God's ready if you are.

Free Haircuts

OCTOBER 12

A barber gave a rabbi a haircut and then refused to accept pay. "I don't charge clergy for haircuts," he said. The next day when the barber arrived at work, he found a loaf of Jewish rye bread on his doorstep.

A few days later, he gave a free haircut to the local priest. One day later, he arrived at work, only to find a bottle of wine left by the priest.

And then he gave a free haircut to the local Baptist pastor. The next day when he arrived at work, he was greeted by fifteen other pastors waiting on his doorstep.

Too often we are like the Baptist pastor, gladly accepting the benevolence of others while not giving any ourselves. God has a special warning for people like that: "Faith without deeds is dead" (James 2:26).

Recovery Step: Nothing will bless you more than helping others experience the same benefits and recovery that you have received.

Plan B

OCTOBER 13

There's Still Hope was never God's Plan A.

There. I said it. What does that mean?

I'm glad you asked. The thing is, God's Plan A was for me to get into recovery thirty years sooner. If I had done that, I would have never lost my pastoral ministry. And we would have never launched There's Still Hope. Twelve books, eleven weekly groups, daily Recovery Minutes, 90-Day Recovery Program, spouse groups, couples groups—none of it would have ever come to be.

But I must say, we are having more fun with Plan B than we ever had with Plan A. Why is that? Because we serve a God of redemption. What the enemy intended for evil, God turned for good.

James A. Yorke said, "The most successful people are those who are good at Plan B." And God said, "See, I am doing a new thing" (Isa. 43:19).

You may have shredded God's Plan A for your life. Don't fret. His Plan B is still more than you could ask or think.

Recovery Step: Embrace the God of Plan B. The God of second chances has a future for you that is greater than your wildest dreams.

The Enemy Will Find You

OCTOBER 14

During a Civil War battle, one of General James Longstreet's officers approached him to say that he couldn't obey Longstreet's order to bring up his men to the line of battle since the enemy was too strong. Longstreet responded with sarcasm. "Very well. Never mind. Just let them stay where they are. The enemy will advance, and that will spare you the trouble."

If we are to maintain sobriety, we must engage the enemies of our recovery every day—temptation, fantasy, past failures, and most of all complacency.

An Alpine guide died on a mountainside in Europe. At that spot a sign reads, "He died climbing." May that be said of each of us.

A. W. Tozer said, "Complacency is a deadly foe of all spiritual growth. Acute desire must be present or there will be no manifestation of Christ to his people. He waits to be wanted."

Solomon was right: "Through laziness, the rafters sag; because of idle hands, the house leaks" (Eccles. 10:18).

Engage the enemy or the enemy will engage you. Complacency is not an option. If your house is leaking, it's time to plug the hole.

Recovery Step: Your problem is not a lack of knowledge but a lack of action. You know what to do. Now do what you know.

Shadows

OCTOBER 15

While preparing for his fight with George Foreman, Muhammad Ali said, "I've seen George Foreman shadow box, and the shadow won."

Often, the shadow wins.

There are fifty-two references in the Bible to shadows. Here's one of those references tucked away in one of the least read books of the Old Testament: "Our days on earth are like a shadow, without hope" (1 Chron. 29:15).

Shadows are dark, but they don't last. They can represent times in our lives when nothing seems clear. Shadows can change the way everything around us appears. But again, shadows don't last.

While you're in the shadow, remember this. There cannot be a shadow without first having the presence of light. The one who said, "I am the light" (John 8:12 ESV) is near, or there could be no shadow.

Recovery Step: If you are walking in the shadow right now, trust in the Light who must be close by.

Create a Better Past

OCTOBER 16

Here's a key to recovery you have never heard before.

You need to create a better past.

We've all heard it a million times: Create a better future. But how do you do that? I suggest that the best way to create a better future is by creating a better past. By that, I mean stay sober for the next twenty-four hours. If you do that, you will wake up tomorrow with a better past. Do that for a week, and your past will be even better.

One of the things that fuels our addiction or our recovery is our remembered past. By creating a past that is full of right decisions, sober living, and spiritual connections, we have something to draw on going forward.

So yes, you need a better future. But in order to have that better future, you need to create a better past.

Recovery Step: Jesus said, "Do not worry about tomorrow" (Matt. 6:34). But he never said, "Take no thought for yesterday." So today, live a sober life, make wise choices, and do the next right thing. In the process, you will create a better past.

The Dried-Up Brook

OCTOBER 17

"So [Elijah] did what the Lord had told him. He went to the Kerith Ravine, east of the Jordan, and stayed there. The ravens brought him bread and meat in the morning and bread and meat in the evening, and he drank from the brook" (I Kings 17:5–7).

Does that sound familiar to your life's experience? Have you been rolling along and suddenly your brook dried up? Business was great until the brook dried up. The blessings were flowing until the brook dried up. Life was easy. Then the brook dried up.

John Bunyon was a faithful servant of God living in seventeenth century England. He preached against the godlessness of his day until the authorities threw him into prison. His opportunities to freely preach the gospel had passed. His brook dried up.

But Bunyon accepted this as part of God's plan. He had nothing else to do in prison, so he began to write. The result was the most read Christian document ever penned, apart from the Bible. *Pilgrim's Progress* has been read by millions of people around the world.

When your brook dries up, remember this: God is still at work.

Recovery Step: When life is easy, when challenges abound, when your brook dries up, get ready. God is still at work.

Frog for Breakfast

OCTOBER 18

Mark Twain is purported to have said, "Eat a live frog first thing in the morning and nothing worse will happen to you the rest of the day."

Moving from a bad yesterday to a better tomorrow requires many things. One of them is the need to relinquish control.

Billy Roberts, mental health therapist in Columbus, Ohio, wrote, "One way to help yourself get through hard times is to let yourself off the hook for things."

Another mental health counselor, Gina Marie Guarino, warns against control: "Hard times come with challenges that are out of your control, and the harder you try to control the outcome of a difficult time, the more stress you are inflicting onto yourself." Did you eat a frog this morning? I suggest two things: (1) give the rest of your day to God, and (2) go brush your teeth.

Recovery Step: Relinquish control to the one who said, "Come to me, all you who are weary and burdened, and I will give you rest" (Matt. 11:28).

Wait a Second!

OCTOBER 19

We serve the God of the second chance. In fact, rarely does a person get it right the first time—in recovery or in life.

James Braddock was a washed-up Depression-era boxer. No one would pay him to fight, and he was living on welfare. Then one night a boxer couldn't get to town for a match, so Braddock stepped in at the last minute. Two years later, he defeated Max Baer for the heavyweight championship of the world.

Life is all about second chances.

Presidents Adams, Jefferson, Monroe, Jackson, Harrison, Buchanan, Fillmore, Johnson, Grant, Cleveland, Nixon, Reagan, and Bush were all elected—on their second try.

Michael Jordan is the greatest basketball player of all time. He was a fourteen-time All-Star, and his teams won six NBA championships, but not until he failed to win a title in his first seven years.

Remember the story of Jonah? "The word of the Lord came to Jonah . . . 'Go to the great city of Nineveh and preach against it'" (Jon. 1:1–2). But Jonah ran the opposite direction. One giant fish later, "the word of the Lord came to Jonah a second time" (Jon. 3:1).

> **Recovery Step:** Your past is no predictor of your future. No matter how far you have fallen, you can still get up. So get moving. You serve the God of a second chance.

The Challenger Explosion

OCTOBER 20

It happened in 1986. I remember it well. On January 28, 1986, the US space shuttle *Challenger* exploded seventy-three seconds after liftoff from Florida, killing all seven on board, including a school teacher who had been selected as the first American civilian to travel in space.

That was a devastating day for America and for my area in particular. You see, the church I pastored at the time was five miles from the Johnson Space Center where each of those fallen astronauts lived and trained. It hit us hard.

God shows up in times like that. "The Lord is close to the brokenhearted and saves those who are crushed in spirit" (Ps. 34:18).

When you have suffered unspeakable grief, do four things.

- Keep trusting.
- Keep moving.
- Keep listening.
- Keep praying.

Recovery Step: In your hardest times and darkest moments, keep looking to God.

Five Friends

OCTOBER 21

Nothing matters more than the people you choose to spend time with. Author Jim Rohn said that we become the average of the five people we spend the most time with.

Solomon concluded, "Walk with the wise and become wise, for a companion of fools suffers harm" (Prov. 13:20).

There are certain people you need to avoid:

- Canaanites: They were always intruding on what the Israelites had.
- Parasites: They will suck the life out of you.
- Termites: They chip away at the work others have done.
- Neophytes: They think they know it all.

If you are to maintain your sobriety, spend time with others who have already done the same. If you want to expedite your recovery, use the flashlight of the gospel to see the kryptonite of temptation. Ask God to provide oversight of what you do, and your recovery will be watertight, but it won't happen overnight.

Recovery Step: Pick five good friends, and your recovery will be dynamite.

The $25 Piano

OCTOBER 22

In 1992, a lady in western Maryland by the name of Ellen Kelly bought an old piano for $25. Twenty-seven years later, she found 110 old baseball cards in it. Among the cards was a Babe Ruth rookie card, which she sold for $130,000.

That old piano was pretty worthless on its own. The wood, keys, all of the components—they were shot, except for the Babe Ruth baseball card.

Our worth is not found in who we are or what we're made of. It's what's inside that counts. Paul said that each of us who are in Christ has the presence of God living inside of us through the person of the Holy Spirit (Rom. 8:9).

And that makes all things possible—including sobriety.

Recovery Step: Walk in the power that you already have.

Knute Rockne

OCTOBER 23

In 1931, Knute Rockne died in a plane crash at the age of forty-three. Having led Notre Dame's football program for the last ten years, Rockne was recognized as America's first great college coach. His lessons are still taught in locker rooms and on football fields today.

Here's just one gem from the legendary coach: "One man practicing sportsmanship is far better than fifty preaching it."

Said another way, "Faith by itself, if it does not have works, is dead" (James 2:17).

Sex addicts are good talkers. We know how to say the right thing to deflect from our behavior. We know how to make our spouse think she's the crazy one. We know how to present ourselves as the person we want others to think we are.

I suggest we embrace Coach Rockne's words, with a slight twist: One man practicing recovery is far better than fifty preaching it.

Recovery Step: Become the person you want others to think you are.

Learn from the Snail

OCTOBER 24

Nineteenth-century preacher Charles Spurgeon taught what he called the lesson of the snail. He said, "By perseverance the snail reached the ark."

Nothing will bring you victory over lust like perseverance. Never give up. Failure is the path of least persistence.

Consider the honey bee. To produce one pound of honey it must visit 56,000 clover heads. Since each head has sixty flower tubes, it must make 3.36 million visits to produce one pound of honey.

A Little League baseball team trailed by twenty-one runs entering the bottom of the first inning. Still, one of the players remained confident. "Why are you so optimistic?" a coach asked. "It's simple," said the boy. "We haven't batted yet."

Your job is simple. Do the next right thing. Then do that again tomorrow. Take small steps—one day at a time. Paul said it like this: "Never tire of doing what is good" (2 Thess. 3:13).

Think of yourself as the snail and the ark as recovery. You can get there. It won't be easy, and it won't come fast. But it can happen if you have perseverance.

Recovery Step: Do one thing that takes you in the right direction today.

Broken Lawnmower

OCTOBER 25

When Bob's lawnmower quit on him, he called the repair shop. He asked the man at the shop what he recommended.

"We always suggest you try to fix the lawnmower yourself first. Only bring it to us if that doesn't work."

Bob responded, "Wow! Thanks for the tip. But does your boss know you're turning away business?"

"It was his idea," said the worker. "We have found that when people try to fix things themselves, they only make things worse. Then, when they finally break down and bring it into the shop, we have a major project on our hands."

Step 2 says, "We came to believe that a power greater than ourselves could restore us to sanity."

Recovery Step: If your "lawnmower" is broken, bring it to the One who says, "Do not fear; I will help you" (Isa. 41:13).

The Man Who Designed the Flag

OCTOBER 26

If Robert C. Heft was here today, he'd say, "Don't let anyone else define your future."

Heft should know. In 1958 at the age of seventeen, he submitted a design for the new American flag, with fifty stars. His teacher gave him a B- for his efforts. Undeterred, he sent his design to the White House. President Dwight D. Eisenhower selected his design from the 1,500 he received.

Heft would go on to become a college professor and mayor. But it was what he did at seventeen that he would always be best known for.

Never underestimate the achievements of your youth. And don't listen too much to the guy who gives you a B-.

The Bible promises, "Commit to the Lord whatever you do, and he will establish your plans" (Prov. 16:3).

Recovery Step: Two things will take you a long way in recovery: (1) start early, and (2) don't let your critics define you.

Running on Empty

OCTOBER 27

"Do not get drunk on wine, which leads to debauchery. Instead, be filled with the Spirit" (Eph. 5:18).

Years ago as I was driving along, I noticed that my gas gauge was on empty. I noticed a convenience store nearby with a gas pump. So I pulled in, swiped my credit card, and began filling my tank. Then I went inside where I bought a soda and talked to the store clerk. After a couple minutes, I returned to my car and drove off. About a mile down the road, I happened to glance down and noticed that my gas gauge was still on empty.

Back at the convenience store, I had done everything I needed to do except the one thing that mattered most. I neglected to squeeze the lever.

In recovery, you can do everything right, but apart from the filling of the Holy Spirit, you will be running on empty. And you will eventually run out of gas.

Recovery Step: Ask God to fill your tank—every day. Don't do another day of recovery apart from the filling and power of the Holy Spirit.

Innocence

OCTOBER 28

Purity is not innocence.

If you define your sexual sobriety by zero thoughts of fantasy, no second looks, and only the purest of motives, prepare to reset your sobriety date—often.

Purity is not innocence.

This is not to excuse any of the above. You absolutely should strive every day to overcome fantasy, second looks, and poor motives. But perfection? It won't happen.

The Bible says, "There is no one on earth who is righteous, no one who does what is right and never sins" (Eccles. 7:20).

Don't let perfection become the enemy of good effort. I like the way Zig Ziglar said it: "Doing your best is more important than being the best."

> **Recovery Step:** No one expects you to be perfect, but we do expect you to remain sober. God's best plus your best makes that possible.

A Reporter's Miracle

OCTOBER 29

Christopher Heimerman is a writer for the *Milwaukee Journal Sentinel*. He checked all the boxes:

- Husband
- Father of two
- Active in his church
- Runner of five marathons
- Celebrated journalist

But there was another side to Heimerman's life. In his own words, "Hours after church, I was often funneling beer or whiskey in the quiet, dark corners of our house. Yet another domino tipped. Another week of drinking every day was officially underway."

Eventually, Heimerman found recovery after he reconnected with God. What came next was hours of therapy, AA meetings, confessing his struggle, and going public with his recovery. For Christopher Heimerman, to find lasting recovery, he had to come out of the darkness.

And that is the promise of God: "The darkness is passing" (1 John 2:8).

Recovery Step: In order to walk in the light, you must come out of the darkness.

Turning Back

OCTOBER 30

It's one of the saddest verses in the Bible: "From this time many of his disciples turned back and no longer followed him" (John 6:66).

In the recovery world, we call that relapse.

We find the following data on relapse from the Recovery Village:

- Following treatment, 80 percent suffer relapses within the first year.
- After two years of sobriety, the relapse rate drops to 40 percent.
- The relapse rate after five years of sobriety is just 15 percent.

The bad news is this: Relapse happens. The good news is: It doesn't have to.

You don't have to turn away—from Jesus or recovery. The key to long-term sobriety is short-term sobriety. And the key to short-term sobriety is what you do for the next twenty-four hours.

Recovery Step: You really have just two choices: move forward or turn back. And I think we both know which is the right way to go.

You're So Vain

OCTOBER 31

Throughout history, pride has been man's undoing. Greece said, "Be wise and know yourself." Rome said, "Be strong and discipline yourself." Religion says, "Be good and reform yourself." Epicure-anism says, "Be resourceful and expand yourself." Psychology says, "Be confident and assert yourself." Materialism says, "Be possessive and please yourself." Ascetism says, "Be lowly and suppress yourself." Humanism says, "Be capable and believe in yourself." Pride says, "Be superior and promote yourself."

But Jesus says, "Be unselfish and humble yourself."

God has always promised blessings to the humble. We read in the Old Testament, "When the Lord saw that they humbled themselves, this word of the Lord came to Shemaiah: 'Since they have humbled themselves, I will not destroy them but will soon give them deliverance'" (2 Chron. 12:7).

You will not come to the beginning of recovery until you come to the end of yourself.

Recovery Step: Come to the end of yourself so you can come to the beginning of recovery.

NOVEMBER

Consider it pure joy, my brothers and sisters,
whenever you face trials of many kinds,
because you know that the testing of your
faith produces perseverance.
Let perseverance finish its work
so that you may be mature and complete,
not lacking anything.

—James 1:2–4

You Already Have Enough

NOVEMBER 1

When God told Gideon to lead his people to victory over the Midianites, Gideon complained that he was the weakest man in the weakest family in the weakest tribe of Israel. Gideon essentially said, "Get someone else!"

To that, God said, "Go in the strength you have" (Judges 6:14).

That is life-changing. "Go in the strength you have." God didn't tell Gideon to wait for more strength or even to pray for more strength.

I hear it all the time. "I need more strength to quit porn."

The fact is, God has already given you all the strength, knowledge, time, and tools that you need. You can walk in freedom if you really want to. But that's the catch. You must really want to.

Recovery Step: Go in the strength that you already have.

The Second Chance Club

NOVEMBER 2

The word on the street is that you've messed up. You have crossed some lines you never thought you'd cross. You have stumbled, fallen, relapsed, and stumbled again.

Welcome to the Second Chance Club. Let me introduce you to some charter members:

- Abraham: He pretended his wife was his sister because he didn't have enough faith that God would protect him.
- Moses: He murdered a dude.
- Jonah: He ran from God as far as he could go.
- Rahab: She made her living as a prostitute.
- David: He committed adultery and had the woman's husband put to death.

What do these five people share in common? They are all in God's "hall of fame" (Heb. 11).

It's time to confess your guilt, grief, and grudges. Surrender them to God. And quit thinking so highly of yourself that you think your sin can outdo God's grace.

> **Recovery Step:** "Forget the former things; do not dwell on the past. See, I am doing a new thing! Now it springs up; do you not perceive it? I am making a way in the wilderness and streams in the wasteland" (Isa. 43:18–19).

Unstuck

NOVEMBER 3

The Tartar tribes of central Asia spoke a certain curse against an enemy. They didn't call for their enemy's swords to rust or for the people to die of disease. Instead, they said, "May you stay in one place forever."

In recovery, it is critical that we keep moving forward. When we quit working the Steps, going to meetings, and making the calls, we get stuck. And before long, we lose the ground we have worked so hard to gain.

The Bible says, "But as for you, be strong and do not give up, for your work will be rewarded" (2 Chron. 15:7).

For most of us, recovery is not a linear journey. There are a lot of ups and downs. It is not uncommon to experience setbacks, especially early in the process. When temptation comes—as it will—the worst thing we can do is to not give in, but to give up.

Recovery Step: Are you stuck in your recovery? Then it's time to get unstuck. Take one short step today that leads down a pathway to freedom and blessing.

The Price of Throwing Christmas Trees

NOVEMBER 4

A woman lost her $823,000 injury claim after lawyers found a photo of her winning a Christmas-tree-throwing competition. Yes, you read that correctly.

Kamila Grabska, age 36, was in a car accident that she claims left her unable to work. When her insurance refused to pay, she sued them for $823,000. Her case was looking good until she entered the Christmas-tree-throwing contest—and won. While claiming she was unable to lift light objects or do any kind of physical work, she seemed to win the sympathy of the court until she started tossing Christmas trees around.

As always, the truth came out.

Jesus said, "For there is nothing hidden that will not be disclosed, and nothing concealed that will not be known or brought out into the open" (Luke 8:17).

We may have never met, but I know something about you. I know that the secrets you are hiding today will be revealed tomorrow.

Recovery Step: Get all the secrets out now. The price of secrecy will only go up.

Prison

NOVEMBER 5

Three men were each sentenced to twenty-year prison terms. Each was allowed to bring one item into their cell that they could keep for the entire twenty years. The first man requested a stack of books, the second requested his wife, and the third man asked for an unlimited supply of cigarettes.

At the end of the twenty years, they asked each man about his prison time.

The first man said, "I read every book and am ready to pursue a successful career."

The second man said, "My wife and I now have five children and look forward to sending them to college."

The third man said, "Does anybody have a match?"

What if we could make you the same offer? What if you could have one thing? What would it be?

There are a lot of great answers. Let me leave you with one.

Recovery.

Recovery Step: Until you have recovery, you will be imprisoned by your own habits. My suggestion? "Flee from sexual immorality" (1 Cor. 6:18).

The Rising Corpse

NOVEMBER 6

Here are just a few strange but true stories.

A man went to a funeral and saw the deceased rise from the casket and stand in front of the church as the attendees entered.

A woman returned home from work one day, only to find the sofa cushions arranged on the floor in the shape of a cross.

Every year, a brother and sister gather to discuss their departed dad on the date of his death. When they do, a mirror shatters somewhere in the house.

How do I know these stories are all true? It's simple. I read them on the Internet.

God's Word is truth (John 17:17). Not the Internet. Not the gossip on the streets. Not even the assumptions you make about the recovery of your husband or wife. The only authentic source of truth is God and his Word. Take everything else with a huge grain of salt.

Recovery Step: It is a good thing to listen to your instincts, but they are not infallible. Try to avoid making assumptions about those around you when you really don't have all the facts.

A New Plan

NOVEMBER 7

There are a lot of interesting strategies that have been implemented in the fight against lust. Some have been found to be more successful than others. And it is my opinion that pretty much any plan that works is a good plan.

But here's one you may have not thought of before. In the words of John Piper, "The deepest cure for lust is to be intellectually and emotionally staggered by God."

Here's another way to say it: In order for you to get over what is to be under you, you must first get under what is supposed to be over you.

Namely, God.

Scripture says it well: "For the Lord your God is God of gods and Lord of lords, the great God, mighty and awesome" (Deut. 10:17).

Recovery Step: Become infatuated with God. Let the knowledge of Jesus Christ and his will for your life become your greatest pursuit.

French Fries and English Muffins

NOVEMBER 8

The English language can be confusing. Consider the following evidence.

There is no ham in a hamburger or eggs in eggplant. English muffins were not invented in England, and French fries did not originate in France. Quicksand takes you down slowly. If vegetarians eat vegetables, why don't humanitarians eat humans? We park on driveways but drive on parkways. A house burns up as it burns down. You fill in a form by filling it out.

I pity the person who has to learn English as a second language. It can be really confusing.

I'm grateful that while something as insignificant as English muffins, quicksand, and driveways can be misleading, God presents himself with great clarity.

The same Bible that says, "God is not a God of confusion" (1 Cor. 14:33 ESV), also reminds us, "The Lord will give you understanding in everything" (2 Tim. 2:7 ESV).

Recovery Step: God is a God of clarity. We don't fall because we don't know what to do, but because we don't do what we know.

Free Concert

NOVEMBER 9

A couple had their car stolen while shopping at a mall. While they were at the police station reporting the crime, the car was returned to the mall parking lot with a note on the windshield.

"I am so sorry for taking your car. Let me explain. While walking through the parking lot, my wife went into labor. We just had to get to the hospital right away, so I hot-wired your car. We now have a beautiful baby girl. Please accept our apologies, along with two first-row tickets to tomorrow night's concert, which we have enclosed."

The next evening, the couple went to the concert. When they got home, they saw that all their jewelry and electronics had been stolen. On the kitchen table they found this note: "Hope you enjoyed the concert."

Most of us don't fall to outright lies. It is the gray area that entraps us, areas of deception.

The answer? Remain diligent.

> **Recovery Step:** The prophet Jeremiah warned, "Behold, you trust in deceptive words to no avail" (Jer. 7:8 ESV). But such trust is not inevitable.

Bad Way to Burn Calories

NOVEMBER 10

There are several ways to burn calories. Swim one hour and you'll burn 250 calories. By riding a bike for an hour, you can burn another 600. Walking an hour will burn 300 more.

If that's not enough, try beating your head against a wall. Seriously. If you strike your head against a wall for an hour, you will burn 150 calories.

Too many of us spend our lives beating our heads against a wall. We keep doing the same things over and over, expecting different results.

William Shatner said, "For years, that is the way I did recovery. I did the same things that never worked, the same way I had always done them. As a result, the sobriety I so desperately needed eluded me like the treasure at the end of the rainbow."

Breakthrough is reserved for those who forget the former things and chase the God who is doing something new (Isa. 43:18)..

Recovery Step: In order to have a break-through, you've got to quit beating your head against a wall. Quit repeating the same mistakes. Do the things you've never done so you can achieve the recovery you've never had.

Super Stitious

NOVEMBER 11

"I'm not superstitious, but I am a little stitious."—Michael Scott (Steve Carrell), *The Office*

We tend to minimize. No one wants to admit to being super-stitious or anything else that sounds really bad. A little bad, maybe. But not really bad.

If you need to lose weight, it's good to minimize. But if you are confronting your hurts, habits, and hangups, minimization is about the worst strategy in any playbook.

Addiction thrives in the darkness, while recovery thrives in the light. Until you bring things into the light, you can't deal with them. That's why Paul said, "The light makes everything visible" (Eph. 5:14 NLT).

You can't treat what you don't see. So quit minimizing. Bring to the light anything that is keeping you from reaching your full potential.

Especially addiction.

Recovery Step: Bring your addiction to the light.

The Strange Funeral of President Hoover

NOVEMBER 12

President Herbert Hoover died at the age of ninety on October 20, 1964, in his apartment in New York City. The next five days leading to his burial were rather typical for a former President.

Until one thing.

At the burial site five days later, there was one aberration from every other presidential burial in history.

No 21-gun salute.

Why? The answer was simple. President Hoover was a committed Quaker, and Quakers are passivists.

Herbert Hoover took a lot of criticism and is widely considered one of our worst Presidents. That Great Depression remains a mark on his record. But give him this: he stood by his principles.

That's how we get well in recovery. We stick with what we believe.

Recovery Step: Paul said it well. "It is for freedom that Christ has set us free. Stand firm, then, and do not let yourselves be burdened again by a yoke of slavery" (Gal. 5:1).

The Tell-Tale Heart

NOVEMBER 13

Edgar Allan Poe's short story "The Tell-Tale Heart" tells the gruesome story of a murderer who hides his victim's body under the floorboards of his house. He is so confident that he cannot be discovered that he invites police investigators into his house and cheerfully answers all their questions, while standing just above the corpse.

Then the murderer hears the sound of a beating heart from below his feet. He wonders why the police don't seem to hear it as the beating gets louder. Though the officers know nothing, the man finally loses it and confesses his crime.

The Bible says, "Whoever conceals their sins does not prosper, but the one who confesses and renounces them finds mercy" (Prov. 28:13).

One of the most unnecessary wars is the one that rages in the heart of a person who has something to hide. They are crippled by their guilt and buried by their secrets. The key to recovery is not living a sin-free life. It is outing our mistakes before they destroy us.

Recovery Step: Confess your sins. Share your struggles. Reveal your past. And in the process, embrace a God who loves and forgives—the creator of the second chance.

Yesterday

NOVEMBER 14

In 1963, Paul McCartney was living with Jane Asher, his girlfriend at the time, at her family's home in London. One night he had a dream of the good times of his youth. When he woke up the next morning, he sat at the piano at the foot of his bed and composed one of his most famous songs: "Yesterday."

Yesterdays always seem better. We remember fondly our first house, first car, and first date. We cherish our childhood memories, easily forgetting much of the pain. We all believe in yesterday.

But God believes in tomorrow. "Jesus Christ is the same yesterday and today and forever" (Heb. 13:8).

Recovery Step: Yesterday is gone. Tomorrow is coming. Today, get ready.

High Places

NOVEMBER 15

"He has a good heart."

We hear that a lot. But is it the "heart" that really matters? Said another way, if the heart is good but our actions don't align with the desires of our heart, what good is it?

We find this revealing description of a little-known king named Asa: "Although he did not remove the high places from Israel, Asa's heart was fully committed to the Lord all his life" (2 Chron. 15:17).

Translation: You can have a "good heart," but if "high places" still remain in your life, you're in trouble.

Asa had a good heart, but his behavior didn't line up. And that wasn't good enough. Likewise, you can have all the right motives, but if those motives don't drive you to do the hard work of recovery, something's not working.

Recovery Step: Oswald Chambers said, "As you cannot take a day off morally and remain moral, neither can you take a day off spiritually and remain spiritual." The same is true of recovery.

Hardship

NOVEMBER 16

If you've been in recovery for more than thirty seconds, you are familiar with "The Serenity Prayer" written by Reinhold Niebuhr. You know the first part of the prayer by memory. But the second part of the prayer is equally impactful.

"Living one day at a time, enjoying one moment at a time, accepting hardship as a pathway to peace, taking, as Jesus did, this sinful world as it is, not as I would have it, trusting that You will make all things right, if I surrender to Your will, so that I may be reasonably happy in this life, and supremely happy with You forever in the next."

My favorite line is "accepting hardship as a pathway to peace." That's my story.

I am the product of isolation and abuse, but God has turned that isolation and abuse into a pathway to recovery. He can do the same for you.

Recovery Step: Say it with me: "All things work together for good to those who love God" (Rom. 8:28 NKJV).

Fully Known and Truly Loved

NOVEMBER 17

One of the hardest things for any of us to believe is that we can be fully known and truly loved at the same time by the same person. Tim Keller wrote, "To be loved but not known is comforting but superficial. To be known and not loved is our greatest fear. But to be fully known and truly loved is, well, a lot like being loved by God."

There once lived a prophet named Micah. A contemporary of the more popular prophet Isaiah, Micah prophesied during the reigns of three kings from Judah—Jotham, Ahaz, and Hezekiah—about 700 years before Christ. Micah lived in difficult times. He preached to a divided people. The Northern Kingdom faced judgment because of their idolatry, and the Southern Kingdom wasn't much better. Micah warned of God's justice while celebrating his love.

Micah pled for his people in the midst of their sins. Hearing of God's pending doom, he said, "Because of this I will weep and wail; I will go about barefoot and naked. I will howl like a jackal and moan like an owl" (Mic. 1:8).

Did you catch that phrase, "barefoot and naked"? Micah was saying, "I'm desperate for a miracle of healing, God. I stand bare before you." By exposing himself, Micah was willing to be fully known. What he didn't expect was that he would be truly loved at the same time.

Recovery Step: Are you fully known and truly loved? Yes, you are. Celebrate that fact by expressing to God your enormous gratitude and fidelity today.

Choppy Waters

NOVEMBER 18

"Joab defected to Adonijah, though he had not defected to Absalom" (1 Kings 2:28 NKJV).

Joab had withstood his greatest test, remaining faithful to King David by not following after the fascinating leadership of upstart Absalom. Yet toward the end of his life, Joab turned away to follow the less attractive leader, Adonijah. He overcame the temptation to follow the man who was poised to take over David's throne and hitched his wagon to a far weaker and more cowardly leader.

Past victories are no guarantee of future success.

In my younger days, I loved to raft over some rather challenging currents, including the Royal Gorge of Colorado. The temptation was always to focus hard on navigating the big rocks in the middle of the river, the sudden drops, and the intense rapids. But it was what came after the drops and rapids that posed the greatest danger—the undercurrents.

Pay close attention to the undercurrents of your recovery. Like Joab, you may have just overcome a mighty temptation. You may have navigated some really choppy waters. But never forget . . .

Past victories are no guarantee of future success.

Recovery Step: Stay focused.

Secret Place of Thunder

NOVEMBER 19

Corrie ten Boom said, "When a train goes through a tunnel and it gets dark, you don't throw away the ticket and jump off. You sit still and trust the engineer."

We are to trust in God, not only in the easy times, but in the "secret place of thunder" (Ps. 81:7 ESV).

I've learned a few things about trusting God in hard times.

- Don't doubt in the darkness what God told you in the light.
- Don't run from the challenge when God is by your side.
- Don't give up on recovery when you've had a slip or relapse.

Recovery Step: If your life has been touched by addiction, you have spent more than your fair share of time in a tunnel. The darkness can be overwhelming. And at times, it seems to have no end. The answer is not to jump off but to keep trusting. Keep going. Keep moving forward.

The Comeback Kid

NOVEMBER 20

Everyone loves a good comeback story. And I can think of no better example of a comeback than Mark's in the New Testament. I'm biased toward Mark for two reasons: (a) my parents named me after him (erroneously thinking he was one of the twelve apostles), and (b) his is a comeback story.

On Paul's first missionary journey, Mark took a wrong turn, leaving the team behind. So great was Paul's disappointment that he never took Mark with him again. But something must have changed because among Paul's final recorded words was this request: "Get Mark and bring him with you, for he is very useful to me for ministry" (2 Tim. 4:11 ESV).

Did you hear that? A deserter, coward, and failure was "useful . . . for ministry." I would argue that God used Mark, not despite his failures but because of them.

If you have taken a bad turn in life, know this: What you see as a dead end, God sees as a glorious detour.

Recovery Step: Let God write another great comeback story—with your name on it.

Take It to the Bank

NOVEMBER 21

You can take God's promises to the bank.

Imagine that I gave you a check for a thousand dollars. Would you withhold your thanks until the check cleared the bank? No, you would express gratitude right away, assuming the check wouldn't bounce, based on what you know about my character.

God's promises are better than our promises. When God says he will do something, you can take that to the bank.

Here are just a few of God's promises:

- He will never leave you.
- Your salvation is secure.
- You can overcome every temptation.

Recovery Step: "Therefore I tell you, whatever you ask for in prayer, believe that you have received it, and it will be yours" (Mark 11:24).

Esther

NOVEMBER 22

The Old Testament tells the story of Esther, a Hebrew woman who became queen and rescued her people. She had three assets that God gave her to fulfill her destiny. She was intelligent, physically attractive, and had an engaging personality. Because of these qualities, "Esther won the favor of everyone who saw her . . . she won [the king's] favor and approval more than any of the other virgins. So he set a royal crown on her head and made her queen" (Esther 2:15, 17).

God gave Esther specific gifts for a purpose. In the same way, God has given you gifts for a purpose. And just like Esther, you have a responsibility to be a good steward of those gifts—not for selfish uses but for the good of others.

Consider three questions today:

1. How has God gifted me?
2. How can I use those gifts to bless others?
3. How can my gifts help me in recovery?

Recovery Step: Identify at least one gift or ability God has given you that you can use to bless someone else.

Arkansas Hunters

NOVEMBER 23

A couple of Arkansas hunters were deep in the woods when one of the men suddenly collapsed. His friend immediately called 911.

"I think my friend is dead! What do I do?"

The operator tried to calm the man down. "Stay calm. The first thing you need to do is make sure your friend is really dead."

After a short silence, the operator heard a gunshot. Then the hunter was back on the phone.

"Okay, now what?"

In life—and hunting—it is important to get to the truth. While the hunter probably didn't do it the right way, the point still holds. Before moving forward, it is imperative to get at the truth of your struggles, addictions, and pain.

Why?

"The truth will set you free" (John 8:32).

Recovery Step: In order to get in recovery, you must walk in the truth—one day at a time.

#1 Key to Sobriety

NOVEMBER 24

I recently read an article called "40 Tips for Staying Sober Under Pressure." I'm sure you can google it. It's right there with other articles on the 11 Tips, 7 Tips, and 21 Tips articles.

But let's cut to the chase. I will give you the #1 way to stay sober. It works every time.

Want it.

Did you catch that? Want it. Be desperate. Stay hungry. Go all in. The most important thing you can do to stay sober is to want it. Really want it.

One of my truisms of recovery is this: If you are 90 percent in, you're 100 percent out.

Before you see a therapist, join a group, or work the 12 Steps, you've got to want sobriety. You've got to want it desperately, passionately, wholeheartedly.

Recovery Step: Let recovery consume your imagination, your heart, and your passion. "Let your eyes look straight ahead; fix your gaze directly before you" (Prov. 4:25). You can be sober. You can stay sober. If you really want it.

Pa Won't Like It!

NOVEMBER 25

A farm boy accidentally overturned his wagonload of corn. His neighbor heard him scream in frustration, and invited him over for lunch.

The farm boy said, "That's mighty nice of you to invite me over, but Pa won't like it."

After a delicious lunch, the man said to the farm boy, "Before lunch, you said your Pa wouldn't want you to take time to eat lunch with us. Where is your Pa anyway?"

Said the farm boy, "He's under the wagon."

The Bible says, "An unreliable messenger stumbles into trouble, but a reliable messenger brings healing" (Prov. 13:17 NLT).

Recovery Step: The story above offers two lessons. First, it is imperative to deliver the right message. Second, you must deliver that message on time. As men and women in recovery, we have an obligation to share our story with the right people at the right time.

Two Success Stories

NOVEMBER 26

It's great to have one significant success story in anyone's life. But two?

Meet Garrett A. Morgan.

The son of former slaves, Morgan conceived and patented the three-signal traffic light in 1923. He had witnessed a tragic automobile accident on a Cleveland street corner and could not rest until he had done his part to make the streets safer for everyone.

But this was his second great invention. In 1911, Morgan responded to a factory fire in New York City that killed 146 people and invented the first gas mask.

Morgan accomplished these amazing feats against all odds. And you can do the same thing. Two amazing success stories are in your future: (a) sobriety and (b) recovery.

Recovery Step: You can do this. God will give you the power to get sober and stay that way. "He gives power to the weak and strength to the powerless" (Isa. 40:29 NLT).

Golf Lesson

NOVEMBER 27

A man loved to play golf. But one Saturday he returned home from a game with a friend much earlier than expected. His wife asked him why his game ended so soon.

The man answered, "Would you want to play with someone who whines about every shot, complains constantly about the course, and makes obnoxious sounds when you are about to make an important shot?"

His wife said, "No, I wouldn't like that."

The man responded, "Neither did my friend!"

In golf—and recovery—we must learn to play with others. God never called any of us to do life alone. Perhaps you need to ask yourself why you are living in isolation.

Recovery Step: The Bible says to "live at peace with everyone" (Rom. 12:18). One of the most important steps you will take in recovery will be the step you take with someone else.

Letting Go

NOVEMBER 28

Most of us aren't very good at letting go. We hang onto old stuff, bad memories, and unmet expectations. Americans are hoarders. That's why there are 32.8 million storage units in the United States, covering over 2.3 billion square feet of space.

But recovery is all about letting go. We must let go of toxic relationships, lingering triggers, and unfulfilled desires. We must quit chasing the rainbow that doesn't really exist, the one "fix" that will finally be enough.

The children of Israel had the Promised Land staring them in the face. But first, they heard this: "Do not take any of the things set apart for destruction, or you yourselves will be completely destroyed" (Josh. 6:18 NLT).

Alexander Graham Bell said it well. "When one door closes another opens; but we so often look so long and so regretfully upon the closed door, that we do not see the ones which open for us."

God has a future for you beyond your imagination. But in order to grasp your future you must release your past. That which threatens to destroy you can do so only on one condition—if you choose to not let go.

Recovery Step: Ask God to show you the one thing you need to let go of, and then start looking for open doors to a better tomorrow.

Sobriety Record

NOVEMBER 29

The record length for sobriety is twenty-four hours.

Sobriety is attained one day at a time. That means you have the opportunity in front of you to tie the all-time record for sobriety. You can do it today. Is it long-term sobriety that you want? Well, let me share a little secret with you.

The secret to long-term sobriety is short-term sobriety.

Forget about next week, next month, and next year. Focus on the next:

- Hour
- Decision
- Temptation

The Bible warns, "You do not know what tomorrow will bring. What is your life? For you are a mist that appears for a little time and then vanishes" (James 4:14 ESV).

Recovery Step: Stevie Wonder was right when he said, "Time is long, but life is short." Focus on today. Tie the all-time record for sobriety. Stay sober for the next twenty-four hours.

John Elway

NOVEMBER 30

On January 31, 1988, the great John Elway took his Denver Broncos to the Super Bowl, only to lose to the Washington Redskins, 42–10. For many, such a blowout would have been devastating.

But another January 31 would eventually come around eleven years later when Elway would redeem himself, leading the Broncos to a Super Bowl win over the Atlanta Falcons, 34–19.

Resilience. Nothing matters more.

The prophet Habakkuk said, "Even though the flocks die in the fields, and the cattle barns are empty, yet I will rejoice in the Lord!" (Hab. 3:17–18 NLT).

Yesterday's mistakes do not dictate tomorrow's outcome. I would argue that you will be better tomorrow, not despite your past but because of it.

Recovery Step: Don't let your past define you. Learn from your mistakes and move forward.

DECEMBER

To improve is to change; to be perfect is to change often.

—Winston Churchill

Greatest Pitcher of All Time

DECEMBER 1

A boy stood on the baseball field and proclaimed, "I am the greatest hitter of all time!" He then tossed a ball into the air and took a huge swing. He missed.

Strike one.

He repeated, "I am the greatest hitter of all time!" Again, he tossed the ball into the air, swung, and missed.

Strike two.

The boy said it again. "I'm the greatest hitter of all time!" And once more, he swung at the ball and missed.

Strike three.

Unfazed, the boy declared, "I am the greatest pitcher of all time!"

The lesson? Don't try to be something you're not.

Recovery Step: Most of us fail because we are playing the wrong game. I suggest you play for an audience of one—the God who looks on the heart (1 Sam. 16:7).

The Running God

DECEMBER 2

Let's play Bible Trivia. Can you name the only time in the Bible when God is shown running?

Answer: Luke 15:20

"So he got up and went to his father. But while he was still a long way off, his father saw him and was filled with compassion for him; he ran to his son, threw his arms around him and kissed him."

Of course, in this story of the Prodigal Son, the father represents God. Let the imagery sink in.

The son wanted to have it both ways—his father's inheritance plus the pleasures of this world. After he had wasted his time and treasure, he hit bottom. Only then did he make his way back home. And the instant his waiting father spotted him in the distance, he ran to his son, giving him a warm embrace.

Never make the mistake of believing your addiction has taken you beyond the reach of God. The moment you get up and return to your Father, he will be waiting, and he will be watching.

And then he'll be running.

Recovery Step: Return to the One who is waiting with open arms.

Robbing the Wrong House

DECEMBER 3

Trying to hurt me by bringing up my past is like trying to rob my old house. I don't live there anymore.

Seneca said, "Every new beginning comes from some other beginning's end."

Carrie Underwood said, "Every day is a new day, and you'll never be able to find happiness if you don't move on."

I offer three suggestions.

1. Quit trying to have a better past.
2. Quit trying to control a better future.
3. Quit listening to anyone's version except God's.

Recovery Step: Give your life to the God of new beginnings. "If anyone is in Christ, he is a new creation; the old has passed away; behold, the new has come!" (2 Cor. 5:17 ESV).

TV Dinners and Pot Pies

DECEMBER 4

We ate them once a week—TV dinners and pot pies. Six nights a week, Mom and Dad insisted that we sit around the table for family dinner at 6:00 p.m. sharp. But once a week, usually when *Batman* was on—we were allowed to eat in front of the television set.

The TV dinner was different from the pot pie. Each segment of the meal—meat, veggies, and dessert—was in its own compartment. But the pot pie had it all thrown in together. The chicken or turkey was mixed with the carrots, peas, and mystery sauce.

There are two ways we can do life: like the TV dinner or the pot pie. But only one is healthy.

Addicts live the life of a TV dinner. Everything is compartmentalized. Each part of life—family, finances, faith, and fantasy—is separated from the rest. That leads to chronic fatigue and constant frustration.

God intended us to live life like a pot pie. We must not separate our secret lives from everything else. It's all interconnected. Proverbs 21:26 (ESV) says, "The righteous gives and does not take back." In other words, we must give it all to God—every day.

Recovery Step: Quit compartmentalizing. Either God is Lord of all or he is not Lord at all. Make him Lord of all today.

Climbing Trees

DECEMBER 5

In December 1874, a snowstorm hit the Western United States. John Muire, a founder of the Sierra Club, left his friend's cabin in the Sierra Nevadas to climb a 100-foot tree from which he would experience the full force of the storm.

Muir made a habit of doing things that took him to the edge of nature.

The Bible tells us about another man who was into climbing trees, but for a better reason.

"[Zacchaeus] ran ahead and climbed a sycamore-fig tree to see him, since Jesus was coming that way" (Luke 19:4).

If you want a fresh encounter with God, you will need to get out of your comfort zone. If you want lasting recovery, you will need to start climbing trees.

Recovery Step: Go to a new meeting. Do a therapeutic disclosure. Become totally honest. Find something you can do to enhance your recovery journey that you have never done before. Climb a new tree.

Focus Less on Recovery

DECEMBER 6

Don't focus so much on recovery.

Huh? I meant what I just said. Don't focus so much on recovery. Instead, focus on the things you must do that result in recovery.

Here's why. Who you are tomorrow is the predictable outcome of the things you do today. Charles Stanley was right: "Where you are today is the result of something you did yesterday."

Your job is to make the next right decision today. Get to a meeting today. Read recovery material today.

As you live in the present, the Word of God will come alive in you. "You will eat the fruit of your labor" (Ps. 128:2).

Recovery Step: Heed the words of Robert Louis Stevenson. "Don't judge each day by the harvest you reap but by the seeds that you plant."

All Things Beautiful

DECEMBER 7

One Sunday in church while I was thumbing through my Bible during the pastor's sermon, I came across this amazing verse: "He has made everything beautiful in its time" (Eccles. 3:11).

Let that sink in. This doesn't say everything is inherently beautiful. It says God takes something ugly and turns it into something beautiful. Something useful. Something good.

I can tick off several ugly moments of my past, but when I think about each one, I see how God turned them all into something beautiful.

God used the death of my dad to introduce me to my future wife.

God turned my day of discovery into a life of recovery.

God took away my ministry to the church in order to create a ministry beyond its walls.

What about you? What is there in your past that, while it was not beautiful, can be useful?

Recovery Step: Let God turn what was ugly into a creation of beauty.

Fake Plants Die

DECEMBER 8

Nothing beats authenticity. Consider the helpful words of humorist Mitch Hedberg: "My fake plants died because I did not pretend to water them."

I'm not sure how that works, but I think there is a subtle message tucked away there someplace.

"Let love be genuine" (Rom. 12:9).

That's what I love about recovery. I find more authenticity in recovery groups than anywhere else on earth. And I've been to a lot of places on earth.

So I know what I'm talking about.

Recovery Step: Step into the light. Live a life of authenticity. Don't let your fake plants die because you didn't pretend to water them.

One Eye Toward Sodom

DECEMBER 9

"Lot . . . pitched his tents near Sodom" (Gen. 13:12).

Here's the story. Abraham's family had outgrown the land where they lived. Abraham had no choice. The family would need to be divided geographically. He offered his nephew Lot several options for where he would settle with his part of the family.

While Lot would never move to the evil city of Sodom (yet), his curiosity drew him in. He settled in an area where he could keep one eye on his family and the other eye on the debauchery of the Sodomites. "Lot . . . pitched his tents near Sodom."

This is where we always get off the rails. The enemy doesn't shout, "Jump all the way into your addiction!" No, he whispers, "Just inch your way in that direction; keep all options on the table." It's called incrementalism. Middle circle behaviors. Inch by inch.

Recovery Step: You can live a life of integrity while keeping one eye toward Sodom. But you can't do it for long.

A Worthy Goal

DECEMBER 10

Two months ago, the Ohio Legislature considered a bill that would criminalize "distracted driving." During a Senate hearing on the subject, a state senator participated in the meeting via Zoom while driving his car. Of course, given the topic of discussion, the senator didn't want his colleagues to know that he was driving, so he put up a background of his office. Rather than seeing the backdrop of a car seat, the other senators saw his bookshelves.

There was just one problem. His seat belt was still in the picture.

Oops.

"Your sin will find you out" (Num. 32:23).

Tennessee Williams said, "The only thing worse than a liar is a liar that's also a hypocrite."

God has a better plan. It's not easy, but it is simple. Be the person you want others to think you are.

Recovery Step: Don't shoot for the elusive goal of perfection. You won't attain it in a lifetime. Instead, shoot for the goal of authenticity. That's a target you can hit today.

Prairie Chickens

DECEMBER 11

The story is told of an Indian brave who discovered an eagle's egg that had fallen off a cliff. He placed the egg with several prairie chicken eggs. When the prairie chicken eggs hatched alongside the eagle's egg, the birds all grew up together. The eagle took on the identity of a prairie chicken.

One day, an eagle flew overhead. The young eagle on the ground looked up with great admiration. Assuming he was a prairie chicken, he wondered what it must be like to be an eagle.

Several years passed, and the young eagle saw another elder eagle flying overhead. This time, that eagle swooped down and joined the younger eagle on the ground. After a lengthy conversation, he said to the eagle who thought he was a prairie chicken, "Don't you know you are an eagle? You were created to fly."

Quit living the life of a prairie chicken, mired in addiction and living in your past. You're an eagle. It's time to soar.

> **Recovery Step:** "They who wait for the Lord shall renew their strength; they shall mount up with wings like eagles; they shall run and not be weary; and they shall walk and not faint" (Isa. 40:31 ESV).

Finishing Strong

DECEMBER 12

On May 25, 1935, the legendary Babe Ruth played his final home game. He had four hits in four at bats, including three home runs.

There's something to be said for finishing strong.

James Dobson wrote, "My legacy doesn't matter. It isn't important that I be remembered. It's important that when I stand before the Lord, he says, 'Well done, good and faithful servant.' I want to finish strong."

Paul said, "I have fought the good fight, I have finished the race, I have kept the faith" (2 Tim. 4:7).

For my fellow addicts, I offer five ways to finish strong.

1. Stay thirsty.
2. Stay focused.
3. Stay connected.
4. Stay diligent.
5. Stay humble.

Recovery Step: You can't go back and design a new beginning. But you do get to design the end game. Starting now.

463 Times

DECEMBER 13

Genesis 4:3 says, "And in process of time it came to pass that Cain brought an offering of the fruit of the ground to the Lord."

That was the first "it came to pass" in the Bible, but not the last. The Bible says it 463 times: "It came to pass."

I have claimed that promise many times in my life. I was declared legally blind at age fifteen. I lost my dad as a teenager. I endured physical and sexual abuse as a child. And each experience "came to pass."

I am also grateful for dozens of kidney stones that "came to pass."

Write this on your forehead: Your present is not your future. Whatever struggles, sins, and setbacks you have experienced in life will come to pass.

Recovery Step: Rejoice in this: Your present is not your future. It will come to pass.

Why People Fail

DECEMBER 14

There is a simple reason many of us don't reach our goal of recovery. We quit too soon.

Thomas Edison was right: "Many of life's failures are people who did not realize how close they were to success when they gave up."

Scaling Mount Recovery will be the hardest climb of your life. There will be many times when you will become exhausted, frustrated, and want to turn back. If you find yourself wanting to turn back today, I ask you to do five things first:

1. Attend one more meeting.
2. Read one more book.
3. Pray one more prayer.
4. Make one more call.
5. Take one more step.

Recovery Step: "Let us not become weary in doing good, for at the proper time we will reap a harvest if we do not give up" (Gal. 6:9). I like the way legendary actress Mae West said it: "You only live once, but if you do it right, once is enough."

Instant Cake Mix

DECEMBER 15

In 1947, General Mills introduced its first instant cake mix. They expected overwhelming success, but the cake mix didn't sell well. The company was confused because it had reduced a difficult task to a mix that only required adding water.

The problem was that the process was made too easy. General Mills hired a marketing expert, Ernest Dichter, to figure out the problem. His conclusion? We bake cakes for special occasions. It is an expression of love. Less effort made it less meaningful.

Recovery takes effort. Rebuilding trust takes effort. There are no shortcuts. Guys, if you are to be the husband your wife deserves, that will require Christlike love followed by Christlike service.

"Husbands, love your wives, just as Christ loved the church and gave himself up for her" (Eph. 5:25).

Recovery Step: Instant cake mix is okay. Instant recovery, not so much. And instant restoration of a marriage shattered by infidelity? It never works.

The Dam Broke!

DECEMBER 16

On March 26, 1913, in Columbus, Ohio, a man was spotted running through town. It was later discovered that he was running because he was late for an appointment.

But out of curiosity, a young boy saw him and then ran behind him to see where he was going. Then others joined in. As a joke, one of them yelled over to onlookers, "The dam broke!"

Chaos ensued. Hundreds of citizens joined the run, fearing for their lives from the flood that would come from the dam that broke.

The fact was that there was no dam to break. The story was carried in the local newspaper, the *Columbus Citizen*, the next day.

Fear can be a terrible thing, and most of our fears never actually come to pass. It's far better to walk by faith and live in the truth.

Recovery Step: "Do not spread false reports" (Exod. 23:1). And learn to walk in faith.

Bless God!

DECEMBER 17

There is this little verse in the New Testament that we often miss. "Jesus said to her, 'Give me a drink'" (John 4:7 ESV). When Jesus made this request of the woman at the well, he was teaching us a bigger lesson.

How many times have we been expecting Jesus Christ to quench our thirst when we should have been satisfying him?

The prayer of millions is this: "God, save me from my addiction. Take away the urges. Forgive me and make me whole."

But what if we took the emphasis off of what we want God to do for us and put it on what God wants us to do for him?

It is in giving that we receive, and it is in pouring ourselves out that we are filled.

Recovery Step: Quit asking God to bless you and start blessing God.

Rebuild

DECEMBER 18

About 750 years before Christ, there was a man named Amos who was a full-time fig grower and part-time preacher. Though he was from Judah, God led him to prophesy to the people of Israel who were living in bondage to a foreign empire. He brought them this message directly from God: "I will bring my people Israel back from exile. They will rebuild the ruined cities and live in them" (Amos 9:14).

Notice the details of Amos's message: "They will rebuild the ruined cities and live in them."

Sometimes when we would rather God give us a new place to live, he says to rebuild what we already have. In recovery, the word is often rebuild, not remove. We ask God to remove us from the pain, addiction, and trauma. God says rebuild.

Recovery Step: Have you been asking God to remove your current situation? Perhaps a better prayer would be to ask God for the tools to rebuild what is left in ruins.

24-Hour Challenge

DECEMBER 19

Rabbi Joseph Telushkin, author of *Words That Hurt, Words That Heal*, states that he asks audiences whether they can go twenty-four hours without saying any unkind words about or to anyone. Invariably, very few people answer yes.

Here's my challenge. Commit to going the next twenty-four hours without doing any of the following:

- Criticizing your spouse
- Complaining about your job
- Criticizing your church
- Using sarcasm in a hurtful way
- Complaining about someone else's decisions
- Criticizing your government

Our Lord's brother James had a keen understanding about the tongue. May his words sink in today. "The tongue also is a fire, a world of evil among the parts of the body. It corrupts the whole body, sets the whole course of one's life on fire" (James 3:6).

Recovery Step: Pray this new form of the Serenity Prayer. "God, grant me the serenity to accept the people I cannot change, the courage to change the ones I can, and the wisdom to know it's me."

Facing Fear

DECEMBER 20

I'm afraid of heights, foul balls at a baseball game, and most Mexican restaurants.

What are you afraid of?

We all have our unique fears, and that's okay. It's what we do with those fears that matters. True courage does not consist of the absence of fear, but in doing what God wants even when we are afraid, disturbed, and hurt.

Let's talk about a fear we don't hear much about—the fear of recovery. For many of us, our addiction has become our most reliable friend. When we want it, it's always there. To live without our addiction and enter a whole new way of life is one of the scariest propositions some of us will ever face.

Recovery Step: May we emulate the courage of the early apostles. "When they saw the courage of Peter and John and realized that they were unschooled, ordinary men, they were astonished and they took note that these men had been with Jesus" (Acts 4:13).

Breaking the Shackles

DECEMBER 21

In order to break the shackles of addiction, you must first break the shackles of shame. This is only possible for the man or woman who is sensitive to the work of the Holy Spirit, for we know that "the unrighteous know no shame" (Zeph. 3:5).

Jesus described the specific work of the Holy Spirit: "When he comes, he will prove the world to be in the wrong about sin and righteousness and judgment" (John 16:8).

How does this work? More importantly, what is our role in escaping the prison of shame?

Jon Bloom, cofounder of Desiring God, has the answer. He wrote, "Like the woman at the well, King David, and the hemorrhaging woman, our shame frequently encourages us to hide in the wrong places." He added that the key to breaking the power of shame is the superior power of humility.

Recovery Step: Humble yourself before God. Then watch the power of shame slowly lose its grip.

Broken Gas Gauges

DECEMBER 22

My first car had a lot of things that didn't work well, including the gas gauge. I had two choices: fix the gas gauge (which would have cost more than I paid for the car) or always be near a gas station.

I chose the latter.

It is important that we stay near our power source. But "near" isn't good enough. Remember this lesson: Proximity does not equal power.

Driving my car near the gas station only matters if I regularly stick the gas pump into the hole in the side of my car. Otherwise, it's like a lamp that is not plugged into the outlet. That lamp is equally useless whether the plug is 6 inches from the power source or 6 miles.

Recovery Step: Jesus promised, "You will receive power when the Holy Spirit comes on you" (Acts 1:8). It is the indwelling Holy Spirit who will give you the power to overcome your addiction, your past, and your pain. Until you are filled with the Spirit, you will never know if you can make it past the next bump in the road. Eventually, you will find yourself driving on empty, out of gas, and powerless to do anything about it.

One Oreo

DECEMBER 23

It's harder to eat one Oreo than none.

Is there something you need to say no to? In many instances, abstinence is easier than moderation. Why? It requires less willpower because you rely on a strong decision-making process in advance. Moderation is a slippery slope. In my experience, it's harder to eat one Oreo than no Oreos. If you feed a craving, it grows.

Think about temptation. We all face temptation. And the temptation is to give in to the temptation just a little bit, hoping the temptation will just go away.

It never does.

So what's the answer? Decide before you have to decide. That way, the next time temptation knocks on your door, you won't have to even think about opening that door because you already made that decision.

> **Recovery Step:** Moderation is a slippery slope. So go all in with God, no turning back. "And may your hearts be fully committed to the Lord our God, to live by his decrees and obey his commands" (1 Kings 8:61).

Home for Christmas

DECEMBER 24

In 1943, Bing Crosby became the first to record "I'll Be Home for Christmas." What you probably didn't know is that the song was written about a soldier in World War II who was hoping to come home to be with his family for Christmas.

History tell us of some other guys who were home for Christmas—the very first Christmas. They were the poor shepherds. "And in the same region there were shepherds out in the field, keeping watch over their flock by night" (Luke 2:8 ESV).

The shepherds were just ordinary guys who were rewarded for staying on task with their ordinary duties—doing the right thing, over and over, in simple obedience to their call. That's how we find the blessings that were realized by the shepherds so many years ago.

Recovery Step: Christmas is about the little things. Do the little things right. Like the shepherds, be where you're supposed to be when you're supposed to be there, and great things will follow.

Christmas Bike

DECEMBER 25

When I was about seven years old, I woke up one Christmas morning to find the bicycle of my dreams under the Christmas tree. I was shocked because I was under the impression that such gifts were reserved for boys and girls who had been especially good that year, which I had not been.

I remember asking Mom why she and Dad had decided to give me the gift I so coveted on a year when I was so undeserving. She said, "Your father bought the bike several months ago before you had a chance to be good or bad."

That's what our Father has done for us. He paid the price for our sin and addiction before we had a chance to be good or bad.

Here's how Paul explained it: "What if some were unfaithful? Will their unfaithfulness nullify God's faithfulness? Not at all!" (Rom. 3:3–4).

Recovery Step: "God loves each of us as if there were only one of us" (Saint Augustine). Celebrate that love today!

Deliver the Cheese

DECEMBER 26

One of the most famous stories in the Bible is that of David and Goliath. You will remember that as a child, David was anointed the future king of Israel. Not long after that, Goliath led the Philistines into battle against Israel. Of course, it was David who slayed the giant, paving the way for a great victory.

But do you remember this little verse? "Take along these ten cheeses to the commander" (1 Sam. 17:18). In obedience to the prophet's command, "Early in the morning David left" to meet the dietary needs of the commander of the army (1 Sam. 17:20).

Here's the point. In order for David to be in the right position to kill the giant, he first had to be obedient in the little things. It was his willingness to deliver cheese one moment that put him in a position to be the hero in the next moment.

The lesson is simple. It is simple obedience today that empowers heroic victory tomorrow.

Recovery Step: Recovery is all about slaying the giant. But start by delivering the cheese.

Why Willpower Won't Work

DECEMBER 27

Willpower won't work.

Most of us have put our trust in willpower—our own ability to overcome addiction. But surrender is the key. That is because prolonged addictive behaviors damage the prefrontal cortex part of the brain, which is involved in problem-solving. Addiction damages the very part of the brain that is engaged in the process of overcoming addiction.

If you have been frustrated by numerous failed attempts at sobriety, take heart. The answer is to recognize your Source. Perhaps you've heard this little verse before: "I can do everything through Christ, who gives me strength" (Phil. 4:13 NLT).

Recovery Step: The future belongs to those who set their sights on what is naturally unattainable. That includes recovery. You can do this. Actually, you can't. But God can.

In the Dark

DECEMBER 28

The Universities of North Carolina and Toronto did a fascinating study of eighty-four people. All participants were given the same set of math problems, but half were placed in a bright room, and the other half were seated in a dark room. The ones in the dark room performed better on the test.

Why? Because those sitting in the dark cheated. They copied off of one another's work.

Jesus said, "Whoever follows me will never walk in darkness" (John 8:12). Notice that Jesus didn't say those who follow him will never fail. He just said that they would walk in the light.

Recovery Step: Perhaps you need to adjust your focus. Yes, you need to avoid relapse and walk in sobriety. But what matters more than how you are walking is where you are walking. Determine today that you will walk in the light.

A Stranger Came to Church

DECEMBER 29

One Sunday, the pastor announced that a special guest would be joining the congregation in mere minutes—Lucifer. He told the morning crowd, "The devil will be here in five minutes. If you want to leave, you'd better leave now."

Five minutes later, the devil arrived, walked into the church auditorium, and faced a room full of empty pews—except for one man.

The devil looked down from the platform and addressed the man sitting on the front pew. "Aren't you afraid of me? Do you know who I am?"

"Sure, you're the devil," the lone congregant replied.

The devil asked, "Then why are you still here? Aren't you afraid of me?"

The man explained, "Why would I be afraid of you? I've been married to your sister for thirty-five years!"

So what's the point of this story? No point. I just thought you could use a good laugh.

Recovery Step: The Bible says, "A cheerful heart is good medicine" (Prov. 17:22).

How We All Learn to Walk

DECEMBER 30

How did you learn to walk? I wasn't there, but I've come to this conclusion: Walking is nothing more than controlled falling.

You learned to walk by learning to quit falling. It was only by not falling that you learned how to walk. No one walks without falling a few zillion times. That's why toddlers are made of rubber so they bounce back when they fall.

Not only do I know how you learned to walk, I know what God wants from you today. "What does the Lord require of you? To act justly and to love mercy and to walk humbly with your God" (Mic. 6:8).

This humble walk can be mastered, but only after lots of falling and lots of encouragement, and by coming to the decision that falling really isn't a sustainable, long-term answer.

Recovery Step: Before you learn how to walk in sobriety, you will fall a few times. And many of us still stumbled while taking our first steps. That's how we learn. And that's how we eventually get it right.

No More Spin

DECEMBER 31

A politician was asked for his opinion of whiskey.

"If you mean the demon drink that poisons the mind, pollutes the body, desecrates family life and inflames sinners, then I'm against it. But if you mean the elixir of Christmas cheer, the shield against winter chill, the taxable potion that puts needed funds into public coffers to comfort little crippled children, then I'm for it."

Most of us have an uncanny ability to spin things in our favor. That is especially true of addicts. Most addicts have mastered the skill of turning every question about their behavior back on their spouse.

One of the first steps toward getting well is to face reality, admit your problem, and quit gaslighting anyone who questions your behavior, lies, or motives.

Recovery Step: Coming clean and staying honest won't be easy. It will cost you in the short run, but it is always worth it. "But even if you should suffer for what is right, you are blessed" (1 Pet. 3:14).

BIBLE REFERENCES

RESOURCES FROM THERE'S STILL HOPE

Books by Mark and Beth Denison

Porn in the Pew
Recovery Rules
Advanced Recovery
Jesus and the 12 Steps
12-Week Partner Recovery Guide
Life Recovery Plan
52 Exercises to Keep Your Recovery on Track
Couples Recovery Guide
90-Day Recovery Guide for Sex and Porn Addiction
Broken Vessels
365 Days to Sexual Purity
Porn-Free in 40 Days
The Daily Walk

Resources provided by Mark and Beth Denison

Freedom Groups for Men
Betrayed Spouse Groups for Women
90-Day Recovery Program for Men
Couples Groups
Advanced Recovery Webinar
12-Step Group
Coaching for Women
Coaching for Men
Daily Recovery Minute Devotions
Daily Recovery Rule Texts
Retreats and Conferences
Local Church Events

www.ingramcontent.com/pod-product-compliance
Lightning Source LLC
LaVergne TN
LVHW020521100826
845148LV00010B/1303
* 9 7 8 1 6 3 2 9 6 9 3 3 0 *